To Heidi and Henry
From Jason

To Victoria and the kids—
Mark, Maddy, Nathaniel, Emily, and Nevin
From David

CONTENTS

CONTENTS

MICHAEL MOORE'S RÉSUMÉ: NOTES ON A LIFE OF SMOKE AND MIRRORS

WORK EXPERIENCE

GENERAL MOTORS, Flint, MI, 1972.

Hired to work on Buick assembly line. Quits in frustration after one day. Later makes a film, *Roger & Me,* dedicated to the takedown of GM and its president Roger Smith.

MOTHER JONES, San Francisco, CA, 1986.

Hired as editor of liberal magazine *Mother Jones.* Begins duties by announcing at his first editorial meeting that he wouldn't have printed a single article that appeared in the last three issues. Fired after a few months in office. *Mother Jones* says, "He was impossible to work with. He was arbitrary; he was suspicious; he was unavailable. He ignored deadlines . . ." Moore rebuts by saying he was "too much of a journalist" for the magazine. Moore sues *Mother Jones* for $2 million. Settles for $58,000, which he uses as seed money for *Roger & Me.*

NADER HEADQUARTERS, Washington, D.C., 1987.

Offered a grant by Ralph Nader's organization to write a newsletter about the media. Asked to move on by Nader's organization, who cited Moore's failure to show up for work. Moore attributes the situation to Nader's jealousy about a book deal Moore had made: "He's never gotten an advance like that. . . . He got really upset."

ROGER & ME, Flint, MI, 1989.

Produces movie about GM layoffs in his hometown of Flint. After the initial wave of praise, critics reveal that Moore had manipulated the facts to create a false impression. Instead of responding to the case against him, Moore rants that the critics and/or their magazines were bought off by GM.

NBC STUDIOS, New York, NY, 1994.

NBC releases his series, *TV Nation*. NBC kills his series, *TV Nation,* after nine episodes. Employees complain about Moore, as later reported by the *New Yorker:* "Little by little, he began to alienate people. He disliked sharing credit with his writers. He would often come in late. He didn't yell at people: if someone said something he didn't like, he wouldn't argue; he would simply not invite the person to the next meeting, or the person would be fired."

FOX STUDIOS, New York, NY, 1995.

Fox releases his series, *TV Nation*. Fox kills his series, *TV Nation,* after eight episodes. Writer's Guild of America called in to arbitrate fees and credit dispute between Moore and his writers.

MICHAEL MOORE'S RÉSUMÉ

MGM/UNITED ARTISTS, Hollywood, CA, 1995.

Release of *Canadian Bacon,* his only admittedly fictional feature film to date. Release of film held up two years while Moore quarrels with the studio.

BORDERS, everywhere, 1996.

Borders bookstores promote Moore's *Downsize This!,* hosting him at book signings and speeches across the country. Moore discovers one Borders store is being picketed over firing of an employee. Moore invites the protestors into the store, hands his microphone over to the employee, and urges his audience to shop for books elsewhere.

SALON MAGAZINE, San Francisco, CA, 1997.

Salon magazine chastises Moore's antics. Moore claims that *Salon* was tainted by Borders, one of their sponsors: "That [Borders] would use this magazine to libel me is a low blow from an otherwise respected bookseller."

BOWLING FOR COLUMBINE, Hollywood, CA, 2002.

Moore edits heavily to shape facts to his preconceived thesis: Heston is a racist; NRA is heartless; welfare recipients are victims. Wins Academy Award. Rather than accept the award graciously, he launches into a tirade. Booed off the stage by many of his ideological peers.

REGANBOOKS, New York, NY, 2002.

Writes *Stupid White Men.* Accuses publisher of censorship. Accuses publisher of plotting to suppress book by not printing and shipping enough copies.

DISNEY/MIRAMAX, Hollywood, CA, 2004.

Miramax, a subsidiary of Disney, gives Moore $6 million to produce *Fahrenheit 9/11*. A week before film's release at Cannes Film Festival, Moore announces that Disney has suddenly refused to distribute the film, and condemns the decision as corporate censorship. *The New York Times* declares that Disney deserves "a gold medal for cowardice." Controversy garners much publicity for the film. Days later, Moore lets a detail slip: "Almost a year ago, after we'd started making my film," he tells CNN, "the chairman of Disney, Michael Eisner, told my agent that he was upset Miramax made the film and he will not distribute it." Another successful publicity ploy accomplished.

INTERESTS:

POLITICS. Successively endorsed Ralph Nader, Wesley Clark, and Howard Dean; Democratic National Committee reportedly considered offering him a lifetime supply of hot fudge sundaes to endorse George W. Bush.

REAL ESTATE. $1.9 million home in New York City; $1.2 million summer home in Michigan.

OTHER MEANS OF INCOME. Denouncing the wealthy; charges up to $30,000 per speech to do so.

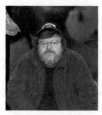

AN OPEN LETTER TO MICHAEL MOORE

Dear Mike,

Here we are again, a year or so later.

What, you don't remember us? We understand how we might've slipped your mind—what with your hectic schedule composing wildly arrogant letters to presidents and other people who actually do things for a living. Or touring Europe to preach resentment of the United States (before jetting back to enjoy the good life here). And, of course, there's the significant amount of time you must spend laughing all the way to the bank.

But we're your "wacko attackos," as you've so affectionately dubbed us. We're among the many who've been keeping an eye on you—and piping up—over the years. And well, we thought you deserved a response to the many unanswered letters you've sent to the high and mighty . . . so here goes.

It all started in March 2003 as we were sitting in our respective homes on opposite ends of the country. While watching the Academy Awards, we saw you take the stage to accept the Best Documentary Feature award for *Bowling for*

Columbine. And like many of the millions of Americans who had also tuned in, we were disgusted and appalled by your shamelessly self-aggrandizing and ironic acceptance speech.

Everyone was waiting for you to thank your team and family, to share the limelight for a moment. But you didn't have it in you. "We live in fictitious times," you bellowed from the stage, knowing that it would make the moment, and indeed the entire ceremony, forever about Mike. Then you summarized your political views: "We live in the time where we have fictitious election results that elect a fictitious president. We live in a time where we have a man sending us to war for fictitious reasons. Whether it is the fiction [*sic*] of duct tape or the fictition of orange alerts, we are against this war, Mr. Bush! Shame on you, Mr. Bush! Shame on you!"

The reaction to your calculated "outburst"—just one episode in a long line from your factory of carefully plotted spontaneity—was immediate and irate, beginning with the audience you addressed. You were roundly and quickly shooed from the stage. This must have been an especially difficult pill for you to swallow, given that you were surrounded, in large part, by your ideological peers. But you had made a foolish, grandiose mistake: You imagined that a few polite handshakes and back pats from L.A. liberals gave you *carte blanche* to make a spectacle of yourself as a grandstanding, blathering, leftist idiot. Understand, Mike: It wasn't that the audience thought your views were wrong. How many Bush supporters and war hawks were there in that Hollywood audience, anyway? It isn't about politics. It's about being a pompous ass.

Outside the Kodak Theater, across the rest of the country, the thundering dismissal of your screed was amplified many times over in offices, at family dinner tables, and around bars.

AN OPEN LETTER TO MICHAEL MOORE

Enter our web sites—Moorelies.com and Mooreexposed.com. Just two small examples of the many web sites where you can find highly critical analyses of your award-winning "documentary," *Bowling for Columbine.*

Thanks to the Internet, the steady stream of insight into the true nature of your work began to pass effortlessly between the mainstream and the underground, between media big shots and regular folks who were sick and tired of standing by while your legend grew unchecked. Seemingly overnight, conventional wisdom about you came under question for the first time. No longer the media darling of your *Roger & Me* days, now much of the coverage about you became more accurate—and thus more angry.

You weren't about to take a hint though.

Instead, your reaction was to dismiss us all—and with malice. You labeled an entire movement looking critically at your work as "wacko attackos," and rather than address our charges, you dismissed us out of hand as "henchmen" of the president or tools of the right wing.

We can get over the almost hilarious paranoia reflected by your response. See, Mike, after the years together, we're aware of the well-worn pattern: People organize and present facts that expose the fallacies of your work, and you reply by characterizing them as "henchmen" and "wackos," whether in interviews, speeches, or on your web site.

The pattern since last year's Oscars is only a heightened version of your longtime modus operandi. You've been loudly condemning a long line of your critics for quite some time now, in exactly the same way, since your *Mother Jones* days in the mid-1980s. You're the King of Deflection and always have been, no matter how long the chorus of criticisms last.

And while your true nature has been revealed several times over your career, like a Democrat caught in a sex scandal, you continue to come back into vogue, stronger than ever. By now, of course, you've got millions on hand (in both cash and acolytes) to keep you afloat.

With your debut film, 1989's *Roger & Me*—a comedic look at the downfall of your hometown—you were savaged by two of film's most respected critics, Harlan Jacobson and Pauline Kael, but it was too late. By the time your misleading editing of the movie was exposed, you were already too deeply insulated by a wave of positive press to suffer any real damage. That didn't curb your reaction (or should we say reflex?) and you were soon shrilly accusing your critics of being part of a General Motors (GM) conspiracy against you.

In 1992, you survived the critical drubbing of your follow-up movie, *Pets or Meat*—which was dismissed as a short and unoriginal rehash of *Roger & Me*—and you even managed to refrain from lashing out at anybody for it. We'll chalk up the silence on your part to a sophomore slump.

It wasn't long before you got your wind back. Your propensity for altering reality served you well in your break into TV. Of course, you had to go to work for NBC, and then Fox Broadcasting—two of the world's largest corporate media conglomerates—but you seemed oddly unperturbed by the hypocrisy. Had you forgotten so quickly that rallying against the scourge of corporations is what made you famous?

In 1994–1995, your show, *TV Nation*, was cancelled by NBC, and then Fox, for low ratings, and your first foray into admittedly fictional film—1995's disastrous *Canadian Bacon*—bombed at the box office.

This time around, you claimed that the film's distributor, PolyGram, buried their own product because they were owned by "weapons maker" Philips. In a way, you had a point: Philips, according to its current web site, is a global leader in the production of such deadly fare as televisions and other home electronics . . . weapons only if they're playing one of your movies, Mike.

After a couple of years, the critical coverage of your public persona began to heighten. In mid-1997, *Salon* magazine fired off a damning indictment of your larger-than-life attitude, and you responded—hey, three guesses?—with a conspiracy theory. Why, one of *Salon*'s advertisers is Borders Books; and the previous year, one of their stores had supposedly "prohibited [you] from speaking at a scheduled event. . . ." Sure, Mike. When Borders isn't selling your books or setting you up for a "scheduled event," they think of little but "how can we get Moore?" (And allowing for the far-fetched idea that Borders did have an ax to grind, *Salon* magazine's editorial content is not dictated by their advertisers.)

The frothing indignation you felt toward . . . well, nearly everyone you'd worked with seemed to fade when you landed a publishing deal, which resulted in your first book, *Downsize This!* The book was a success. Your next step was to go back to your true calling: making movies about yourself. One critic called your 1998 autobiopic *The Big One* "wickedly funny," and we're inclined to agree—that is, if one's idea of a wicked joke is a glib movie made by a narcissistic guy about his tour to promote his book.

Soon enough, we found ourselves in your most prolific period of deception and denial yet. You had more books to sell—and then book sales to brag about, as you're known to do in nearly every interview. We'll give you some credit for shilling, though—after all, one must have to work hard to push a book that is deeply critical of the United States (and even had a chapter titled "Kill Whitey") just a few months after September 11. Of course, we're talking about *Stupid White Men,* which became one of the best-selling nonfiction books of 2002 (although *we'd* argue that it would have been more rightfully categorized as fiction).

Stupid White Men marked more than your return to the limelight. It was also the start of a long and consistent series of Moore thrashings in the press and on the web over your conspiracy theories and drastically oversimplified theses. Kicking off the investigation into *Stupid White Men,* it was *Salon* that got you again this time, in an article contributed by Ben Fritz, one of the editors of the web site Spinsanity.com.

Let's be fair. Mike, we do understand why you dislike *Salon,* and especially Spinsanity.com, for it was the latter who nailed you following the release of your most dramatic piece of fiction yet: 2002's *Bowling for Columbine.* And we know you don't like the many critics who followed suit much better, including our own web sites and others like ours, the *Wall Street Journal,* CNN, and the *London Times,* to name just a few.

And yet you generously continued to give us more material to work with than we could handle! With *Bowling for Columbine,* for example, those who were familiar with the general flaws and factual leniencies in your work had the mother of all targets. So much for your notion that we're just a "nation of idiots"—even your biggest fan base, college students, were starting to catch on.

Your response came like a familiar chorus: The president's goons were after you. "Look, I accept the fact that, if I go after the Thief-in-Chief—and more people buy my book than any other nonfiction book last year—then that is naturally going to send a few of his henchmen after me," you wrote on your web site.

Now let's fast forward to 2004. It's been a year since your Oscar speech, and the spotlight is once again trained on you and your next project, *Fahrenheit 9/11,* which will be your most public effort yet to take down a president.

But this time, we—as two of your many critics—are taking you down first. We're making our case based on a decade and a half of the best and brightest analysis of your product and your persona, from your rewritten history in *Roger & Me* all the way up through your next propaganda reel. We're tackling the four major recurring themes of your career:

1. How you lash out at critics, regardless of the veracity of their criticism, and how you often spin outlandish conspiracy theories around those who don't buy into your act hook, line, and sinker

2. How you preach to a congregation of blind followers, teaching them by your example that facts and knowledge aren't necessary components of rabble-rousing rhetoric, and that it's more important to speak passionately than it is to speak intelligently

3. How you bend the truth to fit your predetermined thesis, creating a false impression for a wide audience that takes in your message

4. How your career and public persona fit the textbook definition of a Narcissistic Personality Disorder, pervading your works with a truly pathological combination of overwhelming egotism and self-loathing

From the early reviews of your career, to the personal accounts of your former fans, to the best evidence of all—your very own work—we're throwing the book at the King of Deflection once and for all.

We've collected more than enough evidence to prove that *you* are the most fictitious character of our times.

Yours,

David T. Hardy
Jason Clarke

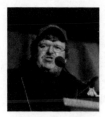

THE PROPHET OF THE LEFT IS NEVER RIGHT

If you're looking for a surefire mode of prediction—on anything from stock prices, to record sales, to presidential election results—well, we've found one. Assume the opposite of anything Michael Moore says, and you've got your finger on the pulse of the future. If he says jump, hit the ground. Take a look at what we mean:

1989: Moore releases *Roger & Me*, an attack on General Motors.

1989–1995: GM's annual profits soar by $1.6 billion.

April 15, 1999: Moore denounces the bombing in Kosovo: "Yes, [Slobodan Milosevic] must be stopped. But bombing the people of his country is exactly the wrong way to stop him. In fact, it has only strengthened him."

June 3, 1999: Milosevic caves in under the bombing and withdraws from Kosovo. He subsequently loses an election, is arrested by his own authorities, and tried for war crimes.

2000: Moore endorses Ralph Nader and campaigns for him.

2000: Nader goes down in flames, taking Gore with him, thus electing George W. Bush.

2001: Moore writes that at least Nader's campaign gave Democrats control of the Senate.

2002: Democrats promptly lose control of the Senate.

2001: Moore criticizes Dick Cheney for being reluctant to sell his Halliburton stock.

2001: Having sold his stock, Cheney saves millions when its price collapses.

September 14, 2001: Moore opposes the Afghan war. "But I beg you, Mr. Bush . . . do not declare war and massacre more innocents."

November 14, 2001: The Taliban collapses, and Kabul falls to American forces.

March 24, 2003: Moore denounces the Iraq war. "Shame on you, Mr. Bush, shame on you!"

April 9, 2003: The Iraqi army collapses, and Baghdad falls to American forces.

2003: Mel Gibson refuses to finance Moore's *Fahrenheit 9/11.*

2004: Mel Gibson produces *The Passion of the Christ,* a film featuring a nearly unknown cast speaking Latin and Aramaic. It grosses over $300,000,000 in its first five weeks.

June 2003: Disney subsidiary Miramax finances Moore.

March 3, 2004: Disney stock values slump, and Michael Eisner is booted as chairman of Disney.

April 7, 2003: Moore defends the Dixie Chicks and proclaims the boycott against them is a failure: "Take the Dixie Chicks. . . . The truth is that their sales are NOT down. This week, after all the attacks, their album is still at #1 on the Billboard country charts and, according to Entertainment Weekly, on the pop charts during all the brouhaha, they ROSE from #6 to #4."

September 26, 2003: The Dixie Chicks announce they have been driven from country music: "Talon News reported on Tuesday that Dixie Chicks violinist Martie Maguire believes the group no longer has a home in country music. . . . '[H]ow can you leave a party now when the hosts had shown you to the door six months ago,' Natalie Maines complains, responding to many of the country radio stations who stopped playing their music after she was critical of Bush on foreign soil."

November 2001: Moore predicts: "[Bush Office of Management and Budget Director] Daniels also owns stock worth between $50,000 and $100,000 in GE, Citigroup and Merck. The chances of this administration allowing a prescription drug benefit for seniors to pass in the next year are about as good as those of me setting myself on fire in front of a Rite Aid" (*Stupid White Men*, pp. 23–24).

December 8, 2003: President Bush signs bill giving prescription drug benefits to seniors.

January 14, 2004: Moore endorses Wesley Clark: "I believe that Wesley Clark will end this war. He will make the rich pay their fair share of taxes. He will stand up for the rights of women, African Americans, and the working people of this country. And he will cream George W. Bush."

February 11, 2004: Clark drops out of race after two New England liberals beat him . . . in southern primaries.

January 20, 2004: Moore hedges his bet, also backing Howard Dean: "Though I am backing Clark . . . the worst thing that could happen now would be for the Dean revolution to come to an end."

February 18, 2004: Dean drops out of race. Dean revolution comes to an end.

October–November 2004: Moore tours campuses, denouncing George W. Bush and endorsing Senator Kerry's candidacy.

January 2005: George W. Bush holds his second inauguration.

December 2003: Moore tours Europe to tout his anti-Americanism.

March 2004: President Jacques Chirac forestalls disaster by announcing his intent to meet with President George Bush and restore Franco-American amity.

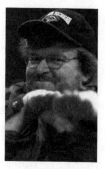

FIRST OFFENSE:
ROGER & ME

What was known until now of Moore's life in the years BC
(Before Celebrity) came from Moore himself. Here's the
fuller picture.

MOORE'S ORIGINS IN FLINT

Throughout his career, Moore has portrayed himself as a
Flint native whose consciousness is shaped by the city's in-
dustrial experiences. "Ben [Hamper] and I both grew up in
Flint, Michigan, the sons of factory workers," he writes in the
introduction of Hamper's book *Rivethead. Roger & Me* constantly hearkens back to Moore's life in Flint. His speaker's
bureau describes him as "born in Flint," his web site calls
him a "Flint native," and his production company's web site
informs us that "Michael Moore was born in Flint, Michigan,
where his father and most of his relatives worked in the auto-
mobile factories. . . ." Asked to describe the source of his empathy for the worker, Moore told *People's Weekly World* that "I
think it's just the function of growing up in Flint, Michigan."
These claims are reflected in almost every biography: Moore

is described as "a Flint native," "the man from Flint," or as hailing from his "hometown of Flint."

In fact, Moore was born and raised in Davison, Michigan, and attended Davison High School. While Davison is *near* Flint, proximity doesn't translate to similarity between the two cities. Davison is the prosperous, white "bedroom town" of the area, largely inhabited by management, not labor. Davison's median household income is one and a half times that of Flint's, and its median house value is just over twice that of Flint's. Davison's 2000 unemployment rate was a minuscule 4.6 percent, a third that of Flint's, and its poverty rate is half of the national average. Davison is also lily-white to a staggering degree: African-Americans make up only one-half of one percent of its population.

1976–1986: EARLY INDICATIONS

After his freshman year of college, Moore dropped out to found a left-leaning newspaper, the *Flint Voice*. On the home page of his film production company's web site, we are informed that "At 22, Moore founded and for 10 years edited the *Flint Voice* (later the *Michigan Voice*), one of the nation's most respected alternative newspapers." The speaker's biography he uses for his college tours tells students the same.

A bit of inquiry showed that this claim is, to say the least, gilding the lily. Even by the standards of the alternative media, both newspapers were tiny players of mediocre quality. They were small (about 20 pages), biweekly publications which eked by on benefices from a handful of wealthy donors.

Worse, they were rather dull. The July/August 1984 *Michigan Voice* consisted of little more than a page listing names of tax resisters, a long article on Ben Hamper's visit to the Auto-World theme park, one by Holly Near on her wonderful visit to Nicaragua, an article on Bruce Springsteen, and some movie reviews—hardly the amusing muckraking one expects from an alternative paper. At times, one suspects Moore was reduced to recycling old material when copy ran short. The Auto World theme park was the subject of five largely repetitive articles in 1981, 1982, and 1984. In short, the *Michigan Voice* and the *Flint Voice* were not exactly home run hits in the American alternative press.

During this period, Moore made some crucial connections. A group of Flint community activists had taken on General Motors on several fronts, and Ralph Nader had joined forces with them, to the point of assigning staffers to live and work with them in Flint and in Detroit. Nader himself was working on a book, one of whose themes was a none-too-flattering personalization of Roger Smith, GM's top executive. (Nader's concept was that, rather than blaming impersonal firms for their harmful conduct, one should understand that the conduct was the product of specific human beings and their choices.)

The activists contacted Moore in hopes of adding his underground newspaper to their coalition, and introduced him to Nader when he visited Flint to speak on how they should personalize Roger Smith rather than pressuring GM as a corporation. One of their number, Mike Westfall, was a union activist trying to find funding for a documentary on GM's practices, the proceeds from which would be used to benefit Flint. Westfall's concept was given to Moore in the hopes his connections would be useful in finding the required assistance. "We had major, major plans back in 1985 to do a movie using the same material that Moore used," Westfall would later note, "the difference is the money was to go back to the community—every dime of it." Westfall got Moore into GM shareholder meetings where community members questioned Smith and asked that he meet with them on key issues. Moore, however, found other opportunities.

It was time to leave Flint, the supposed hometown that Moore has since portrayed as his Xanadu, akin in reverence and misery to the famous mansion of Citizen Kane. In 1986, Moore set out for San Francisco, an ideal place for his musings, where he was picked (above an internal candidate) to be the savior and next editor of the leftist magazine *Mother Jones.* His star was on the rise.

But within a few months, *Mother Jones* canned him. The publisher described Moore as "arbitrary; he was suspicious; he was unavailable." Moore's response was a harsh one: He immediately sued the magazine for $2 million, claiming the parting had occurred over ideological differences.

To make his case, Moore immediately went to the streets. The former *Mother Jones* employee who had been passed over for Moore's job described how the recently fired provocateur stood on the front steps of San Francisco's City Hall to assail the magazine. To make him go away, *Mother Jones* reluctantly settled his $2 million claim out of court for $58,000.

Who was the former employee who'd been passed up in favor of Moore? He was none other than David Talbot, who in 1996 founded the influential and hugely popular magazine *Salon.* And how did he come to relate this story about Moore's early example of overblown grandstanding? Not surprisingly, the issue surfaced more than ten years later, in 1997, when Moore wrote an angry letter to the magazine following the publication of an article that dared to criticize him, detailing his now legendary record of outbursts. This time, Moore's conspiracy theory suggested that *Salon*'s editor had surfaced to whack him for a relatively insignificant (to all but Moore) occurrence a decade earlier.

1987–1988: THE LOST YEARS

With his career at *Mother Jones* at a dead end, Moore returned to Flint, but not for long. In 1987, settled in Washington, D.C., Moore started a weekly newsletter, "Moore Weekly," which was partially funded by Ralph Nader's organization. Unsurprisingly, before long the duo had a falling out. In Moore's version of events, the firing was fueled by Nader's jealousy over a $50,000 advance Moore had been offered to write a book about GM. "He'd never gotten an advance like that," Moore later told the *New Yorker*. "He got really upset." (Nader's office contended that Moore was told to move out because he was spending more time in Flint than on the newsletter.)

Moore's career then took an unusual turn: toward filmmaking. During his previous Flint sojourns, he had become familiar with Mike Westfall's proposal for a documentary on General Motors' practices and how they harmed the community, and with Nader's idea of personalizing corporate executives, in particular GM's Roger Smith. While working in Nader's operation, friends of Westfall had discussed the potential such a documentary would have, and how the story could be told with humor. Moore saw the potential and began filming.

Eager to assist, Westfall provided Moore with hundreds of pages of his own research, and again got him into a shareholders' meeting, where Moore questioned Roger Smith extensively on camera. Later, Moore got to question Smith during a press luncheon and on an exhibit floor. Moore also gathered footage of Westfall and other activists. All anticipated a documentary on the community's conflict with General Motors.

Somewhere along the line, however, the theme began to change. The story of the activists vanished, as did all acknowledgment of their aid and of Westfall's ideas. The theme would now be Moore's single-handed and heroic crusade. The title summed it up: *Roger & Me*. Since its running joke would be Moore's unsuccessful attempts to interview Roger Smith, the footage of him doing just that would likewise be deep-sixed.

After the film became a hit, Moore spent a good deal of time denying the aid of Mike Westfall and the others. On live television, Phil Donahue asked, "But you got a lot of help from—and under way here in Flint, among others, Mike Westfall, a proud UAW member, Jim Musselman, an attorney, drew up the idea for a film about what's happening here." Moore snapped back, "Oh, that's not true. Oh, they lied." He claimed that, "Attorneys from Ralph Nader's office hand-delivered a statement to you today saying that these people are out on a limb, that the Nader office supports this film." When Nader's office denied sending any such letter, Moore proclaimed in the *Flint Journal* that "they want money and they're trying to extort it from me." Needless to say, the millions that the film earned did not go back to the community, save for a trifling amount: Moore proudly told Donahue that he did demand that the distributor pay the rent for the four evicted families depicted in the film.

1989: *ROGER & ME*

Roger & Me was both the brilliant beginning and nearly the end of Moore's career as a filmmaker, landing him squarely in the national spotlight, but also in hot water with critics, the Academy, and even the courts. Moore's fans maintain that the film was "notoriously snubbed" for the Oscar. There's a bit more to it than that.

The plot of *Roger & Me* was intentionally simple: Moore is an Everyman, a stand-in for the "little guy," who pursues Roger Smith—then president of corporate behemoth General Motors—so that he can accompany Smith on a day-long tour of Flint, assessing the human impact of mass layoffs by the automaker.

According to the film, the catalyst for his dogged pursuit was that GM, in late 1986, closed many manufacturing plants in Flint, Michigan, and left 30,000 people jobless. The layoffs had the usual results: a ruined local economy and a soaring crime rate. At a GM stockholders' meeting, Moore finally gets Smith on camera—whereupon the viewer feels shocked, even angry, to watch a GM employee shut off the microphone after Smith abruptly ends the meeting, presumably to avoid Moore's tough questions.

Along the way, Moore evolves the film into a study of Flint's class warfare. The impoverished are evicted (though only one of the four families depicted were former GM employees), while Flint's wealthy party away at the city's annual Great Gatsby Ball. In the film, the city's response to economic and social disaster is brainless. It pays a TV evangelist, Reverend Robert Schuller, to come to town and fire up the people. The city also brings in Ronald Reagan, who buys pizza for some of the unemployed and suggests that they move to places where jobs can be found. While he is eating, someone steals the restaurant's cash register. The city builds a Hyatt Regency, an automobile-themed amusement park, and a Water Street Pavilion to try to make the depressed and depressing city a tourist haven. All these efforts, of course, fail. The key to Moore's theme is the timeline he charts. He positions each of the city's initiatives as a lame response to the GM layoffs.

Critical response to the film during the fall of 1989 was overwhelmingly positive: One magazine writer admitted to not having seen the film—but nevertheless managed to tout its powerful message. One critic, however, wasn't satisfied to rest on hype, and he decided to look just a bit deeper.

Harlan Jacobson was editor of *Film Comment* magazine at the time, and he had done a bit of digging. When he finally landed an interview with Moore, his questions quickly had the filmmaker in a corner. "When did Auto World open?" Jacobson asked Moore. "Autoworld opened July 4, 1984." And when did it close? "January 6, 1985." The Hyatt? "The Hyatt opened in 1982." The Pavilion? "December of 1985."

All seems fairly innocuous, until you realize that the big layoffs that decimated Flint occurred in May and December 1986—*at least a year after* many of the events Moore described as the city's *responses* to the crisis.

It was a shocking confession from a director who up to that point had been the improbable but loveable darling of the nation's movie industry. A major thesis of Moore's documentary was based on an invented timeline.

Moore's interview with Jacobson quickly went downhill from there. Ronald Reagan's visit had been in 1980, as a candidate rather than as president, and the cash register was actually stolen two days before. The televangelist had been brought to town in 1982. Moore's feeble justification: "I didn't say it was done post-1986 . . . it happened during the same decade . . ."

The Jacobson interview, which appeared in the November/December 1989 issue of *Film Comment*, marked Moore's first time in the national spotlight as a filmmaker. Here he started a trend that he would carry throughout the remainder of his career: Rather than address questions about his work seriously, Moore reacted quickly and violently, ignoring any questioning of the facts and instead immediately accusing his critics of being part of wild conspiracies to discredit him.

With *Roger & Me*, Moore's equivocations are as amusing as his movies. Answering Jacobson, Moore gives as much of a concession as you're going to get: "Okay, so you can say that the chronology skips around a bit," he says, in an understatement on par with the suggestion that Antarctica is a bit chilly in the winter. Moore continues, moving from the specific to a restatement of his larger theme: "This movie is about essentially what happened to this town during the 1980s . . . so everything that happened, happened." Finally, he starts to get a bit testy with Jacobson, revealing what would soon be seen as his trademark paranoia: "You've bought into their bullshit. . . ."

Whose bullshit, we may never know, for here Moore's charge is left vague. But because Jacobson's article is widely regarded as the first piece to take a critical look at *Roger & Me*, Moore swung back that a conspiracy was afoot.

Moore's attack was not directed at Jacobson, but at *Film Comment*, which had supported the film during its initial run. In a 2002 article on his web site, Moore had apparently forgotten the magazine's past support (no shock there) and decided that they were also in on the ruse: "*Film Comment* is a publication of the Film Society of Lincoln Center. Lincoln Center had received a $5 million gift from GM just prior to its publishing of the piece trashing *Roger & Me*. Coincidence? Or just five big ones well spent?"

The matter is further complicated when you consider evidence that perhaps the reverse is true. After Jacobson's piece appeared in *Film Comment*—the magazine's Lincoln Center ownership had been extremely supportive of *Roger & Me*—Jacobson was fired.

But the damage was already done: Jacobson had pinned Moore to the wall, and any chance that *Roger & Me* stood for an Academy Award nomination had now vanished, along with the credibility of Moore's film in the eyes of many.

But was *Roger & Me* even a documentary in the first place? Moore complained during his interview with Jacobson, "[Y]ou are trying to hold me to a different standard than you would another film . . . as if I were writing some kind of college essay." No, Jacobson made clear, he was simply judging *Roger & Me* against long-held documentary film standards—to which Moore blurted out, "because you see this primarily as a documentary."

And what did Moore see it as? "I think of it as a movie, an entertaining movie . . . An entertaining movie like *Sophie's Choice*."

Good-bye, Best Documentary Oscar. Hello, recurring theme of wild accusations.

Moore never seriously addressed a single inquiry into the film's veracity when it was released; why would anything change all these years later?

Other reviewers, though, joined in. The *Los Angeles Times* repeated Jacobson's findings, adding that footage of houses in Grosse Pointe was actually shot in Flint, and a scene supposedly shot in Flint was actually filmed in Detroit.

Even GM President Roger Smith got into the act, pointing out that while Moore shows himself trying to track Smith down at the Waldorf Astoria in New York City and at the Grosse Pointe Yacht Club, those on-screen efforts were destined to fail.

"I've never stayed at the Waldorf (Astoria Hotel in New York); I don't belong to the Grosse Pointe Yacht Club (just outside Detroit)," Smith told the *Los Angeles Times.* "Obviously, he had to know that he wasn't going to find me in any of those places. . . ."

Jacobson's article also provided inspiration for legendary film critic Pauline Kael, whose review in the *New Yorker* denounced *Roger & Me* as "shallow and facetious, a piece of gonzo demagoguery that made me feel cheap for laughing."

Moore's response to Kael demonstrated what was becoming his standard three-pronged counterattack to criticism of his truthfulness. On his web site, he assured his followers that the critiques just weren't true, suggested there was a conspiracy at play, and demeaned the reviewer. "She wrote that I had rearranged the chronology, that places like Auto-World were built before the GM layoffs. She wrote that a few things in the film never happened, like the cash register being stolen when Reagan visited a restaurant in Flint," Moore wrote. Then, ignoring the fact that he'd conceded all of these points during his interview with Jacobson, Moore continued: "Her complete fabrication of the facts was so weird, so out there, so obviously made-up, that my first response was this must be a humor piece she had written." He closed with the note that the "establishment leaders" must have conspired to con "an elderly lady penning her last reviews from her rural home" into bashing his movie.

MORE FALLOUT

Though Moore has claimed on more than one occasion that he's never been sued over the integrity of his work, he surely must recall Larry Stecco.

The legal problems began when he filmed Stecco, a Democrat and an attorney well known for his pro bono activism for Flint's poor—in short, the type of fellow Moore is supposed to like. In fact, Stecco had even helped Moore out when he was a young activist serving as editor of the *Flint Voice.*

Unfortunately for Stecco, though, Moore's loyalties fell by the wayside while filming *Roger & Me.* It was an early example of what would become a trend: Moore's willingness to sacrifice people for the sake of getting the right sound byte or shot he needed to fill in his scenes. Having already depicted the misery of Flint's unemployed with wit and understated rage, Moore then needed visual evidence to demonstrate the callousness of its wealthy.

During the filming of *Roger & Me,* Moore learned of the "Great Gatsby Party," a fund-raising event which attracted well-to-do attendees dressed in snazzy 1920s outfits. Moore showed up, and hit a goldmine of material. Plates were heaped with food, and people actually dared to pretend to be like the vacuous rich of the roaring 1920s. For the event, several Flint residents—some of them unemployed, thanks to the GM layoffs—were hired to pose as living statues for the extravagant affair.

And there was his buddy Larry Stecco, with his date for the evening, Susan DeCoutval!

Moore asked Stecco if he would care to be interviewed on a film Moore was working on, a film that would help Flint. Stecco was happy to agree. Following on what he thought Moore wanted for the segment, Stecco praised Flint: It was a great place to live and had ballet and hockey.

And when *Roger & Me* came out, Stecco found himself portrayed as a crass and moronic rich guy. After showing some moving scenes depicting the sad lot of Flint's poor, Moore somberly intoned that ". . . meanwhile the more fortunate of Flint were having their annual Great Gatsby Party." As Moore spoke, over the background of languid music, a filler scene from a polo game was shown. The movie then segued into the Great Gatsby scene—the party, the enormous plates of food, blacks hired to pose as living statues—and Larry Stecco talking about what a wonderful place Flint was.

Although no specific point was spelled out on camera, the inference had been made—these rich people were living the high life, without a social conscience. And the inference had been made at the expense of Moore's (former) friend.

After seeing the film, a furious Stecco sued Moore for false light invasion of privacy. In a false light claim, the plaintiff, Stecco in this instance, asserts that he has been portrayed as something he is not. In 1993, a jury ruled in favor of Stecco and awarded damages, which Warner Brothers, distributor of *Roger & Me,* paid. (It would not be Moore's last brush with the courts. In the mid-1990's, one segment of his *TV Nation*—a comedic news magazine—ended with Moore's producer getting popped with a $4.5 million jury verdict for defamation. This verdict was later reversed on appeal.)

Summarizing Moore's ability to misrepresent his subjects, Pauline Kael famously wrote: "The picture is like the work of a slick ad exec. It does something that is humanly very offensive. *Roger and Me* uses its leftism as a superior attitude."

Regardless of the quality of the work or the critical response, Moore certainly made the most of that first film out of the gates. *Roger & Me,* fifteen years later, still survives as his seminal work. To his fans, it is his first proof of genius; to his critics, his first offense in a career of serial mendacity. It also marks the birth of a powerful public persona: the everyday schlub who asks tough questions of the rich and powerful on behalf of the little guy. Moore had found his appeal. He had also found a go-to response for dealing with criticism of any kind: assailing the person questioning him. In the years to come, these virulent counter-attacks became a consistent coda used by Moore in the media.

STUPID WHITE MEN:
THE GOSPEL ACCORDING
TO MICHAEL

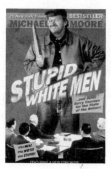

For the briefest moment, the title stirred our hopes that Moore's work might be autobiographical and self-critical. Alas, it proved to be just one more chapter in the Gospel According to Michael.

The title plays to that all-too-human drive to feel superior to others—a powerful rallying cry throughout history. It's powerful enough to fuel major political movements: The Know-Nothings of the 1850s united over their imagined superiority to immigrant Germans and Italians; the segregationists of the next century united over their imagined superiority to blacks. It's a drive that can overcome all sense of reality. In the 1930s, after all, millions were persuaded that tall, blond, Germans were an innately superior race—never mind that the person doing the persuading was neither tall nor blond nor German. As Hitler himself remarked: Anybody will believe a lie if it is big enough.

Most of Moore's productions, both filmed and written, center on Moore showing off how intelligent and sincere he is, in contrast to the nasty, foolish people he attacks "on behalf of the nation." As a result of this construction, the real emotional appeal to the viewer or reader is: Follow Moore, identify with Moore, and you, too, are superior to these often powerful *but really ignorant* people. Or, more simply: *You are not the loser— they are! Stupid White Men* was a perfect choice for a title. And the content also fit the bill—a $25 course in self-esteem for, well, embittered losers.

Chapter 1 of *Stupid White Men* explains how the entire presidential cabinet is inferior to the reader.

Moore lists them all. Dick Cheney, chief of staff to President Ford, defense secretary to George Bush, now vice president: "Bah," says Moore. In between these illustrious posts he was head of Halliburton, which had dealings with Iraq.

John Ashcroft, former U.S. senator, now attorney general: Moore positions him "to the right (if such a thing is possible) of the National Rifle Association when it comes to gun control" since he ordered that background checks of gun buyers, required by the Brady Act, be destroyed within twenty-four hours. What Moore doesn't explain is that the Brady Act itself commands that where the buyer passes the background check, the background check system shall "destroy all records of the system with respect to the call (other than the identifying number and the date it was assigned) and all records of the system relating to the person or the transfer." Ashcroft's command was intended to uphold the spirit of the law.

Gale Norton, Secretary of Interior, a woman who raised herself by her bootstraps, rising to attorney general of Colorado, and then secretary of the interior: "Bah," Moore scoffs. Why, she "helped the State of Alaska challenge an Interior Department fisheries law. She has declared the Endangered

Species Act unconstitutional and written legal opinions against the National Environmental Protection Act." In reality, though, the Interior Department doesn't enact fisheries laws, Congress does, so presumably the challenge was to some regulatory application of them, namely, whether it complied with the statute. (Notice Moore doesn't mention who won that argument.) It would make little sense to write a "legal opinion against" a statute.

Moore gets to Colin Powell next, a combat veteran, general, chairman of the Joint Chiefs of Staff, a key aide to the secretary of defense, and secretary of state. Then he's onto Condoleezza Rice, former provost of Stanford and current national security advisor. With these targets, Moore faces an uphill battle.

He makes a game try at them both: Powell sat on the board of Gulfstream, a company which makes jets for "Hollywood honchos and foreign governments like Kuwait and Saudi Arabia," and Rice, as a former director of Chevron, has an oil tanker named after her. How Moore can see these scraps of information as compelling indictments is beyond us.

The rest of his criticisms are almost too simpleminded to dignify with a rebuttal. Moore, for example, condemns cabinet member after cabinet member for holding positions on the board of this or that large corporation. Hint to Mike: When you're picking people to lead governmental units with tens of thousands of employees, and billions in the budget, presidents tend to look with favor on people who have managed big things. Hope we haven't disclosed any classified personnel secrets here.

Moore really hits stride by Chapter 5, which begins, as usual, melodramatically: "DO YOU FEEL like you live in a nation of idiots? I used to console myself about the state of stupidity in this country by repeating this to myself: Even if there are two hundred million stone-cold idiots in this country, that leaves at least eighty million who will get what I'm saying . . ."

It's a jarringly derisive statement from one who claims to be a spokesman for "the people," but it suits perfectly the real theme of the Gospel According to Michael. According to Moore, the entire nation is composed of morons. "Buy my book," implies Moore, "and you have proven your superiority." Ka-ching! Feel better now?

Indicting the entire nation (or at least those who don't buy his book) as uniformly idiotic is certainly an attention-getting approach, and Moore half-heartedly backs up his claim with proof. He writes: "There are forty-four million Americans who cannot read and write above a fourth-grade level—in other words, who are functional illiterates. How did I learn this statistic? Well, I *read* it."

Moore should have read better. His endnotes attribute the figure to the U.S. Department of Education's National Adult Literacy Survey. Yes, that survey found that 40–44 million Americans performed in the lowest level of literacy. But the survey doesn't end there. In the next paragraph, it goes on to note that 25 percent of the people who scored in the lowest literacy category were immigrants who have learned little or no English. And in classic Moore fashion, he also fails to disclose that nearly 19 percent of the group he includes in the uneducated masses are actually people who have "visual difficulties that affect their ability to read print."

Surprise: Functional English literacy is not high among the blind, and people learning to speak English may be highly educated, but only able to read their native language. This hardly makes the United States a nation that, writes

Moore, "GOES OUT OF ITS WAY TO REMAIN IGNORANT AND STUPID."

(*Note:* The capitalization above is original; Moore loves the cap lock key more than anyone outside a jail cell.)

And let's face it—functional literacy is a worldwide phenomenon, a problem far from unique to the United States. A UNESCO survey found that 21.8 percent of those in England and Wales, and 22.6 percent of those in Ireland performed in the lowest category of literacy. The U.S. figure was 20.7 percent. Conversely, when we look for percentages of adults who read at the highest level of skill, the U.S. figure is 21.1 percent, compared to 16.6 percent in the United Kingdom and only 13.4 percent in Germany. Some nation of idiots we are.

Moore's "you're not a loser, everyone else is, especially the powerful" message has been taken to an international plane. In his appearances abroad, he simply changes that to "Your nation isn't a has-been; mine is." He illustrates this with a gimmick, asking for volunteers from the audience to represent the least intelligent local and the most intelligent American present. Each is asked questions about the other's country—its capital, national leader, and so on. The American generally loses. Of course, what this parlor trick really reflects is that "Washington, D.C." and "George W. Bush" are better known worldwide than are the capital of Canada or the chancellor of Germany.

Next, Moore moves on from reading to geography, another area where he claims Americans are woefully ignorant, while the rest of the world basks in serene and complete knowledge. A standard Moore pitch consists of invoking a *National Geographic* poll that shows that most young Americans couldn't locate Iraq on a map, and then using that seemingly disheartening statistic to flatter by comparison whatever overseas audience he is currently sucking up to. For example, he told a London audience that "[t]he dumbest Brit here is smarter than the smartest American."

Moore never mentions that in announcing the results, the National Geographic Society acknowledged that the survey found that "young adults worldwide are not markedly more literate about geography than the Americans." It backed up this statement with figures that showed fewer than 25 percent of young people worldwide could locate Israel on a map, and only about 20 percent could locate Iraq.

And in fact the world record on geographical foul-ups comes from the nation that Mike, in *Bowling for Columbine* and numerous speeches, holds out as his utopia. The Canadian Broadcasting Corporation has a granite map of North America on the floor of its lobby. A few minor problems: It shows Vancouver Island as a peninsula and has no trace of the Queen Charlotte Islands. In compensation for that loss, it gives Canada the state of Alaska. As the *Ottawa Citizen* reported, "This isn't the first time a bold new geography has been created for the North American continent. In July, the inaugural issue of the Canadian Tourism Commission's magazine, *PureCanada*, contained a map that eliminated Prince Edward Island, Labrador, Halifax and Fredericton." It added that another map, at the Ottawa International Airport, readjusted the United States, locating Atlanta's airport in the middle of Alabama, and Chicago's in Wisconsin.

To be fair, the remainder of *Stupid White Men* is thoroughly humorous, although much of the humor is unintentional. To read it without guffaws, one must suspend disbelief, not to mention common sense. We'll take the book's more out-rageous commentaries one by one.

AMERICANS ARE DYING OF MAD COW DISEASE AND NOBODY KNOWS IT

On page 137 of *Stupid White Men*, Moore latches on to an easy means of stirring up fear and makes the most of it. This time around, it's the facts about mad cow disease that will be bent to his theories. He writes, "Americans are not immune from this deadly disease. Some experts estimate that some 200,000 US citizens diagnosed with Alzheimer's may in fact be carrying the alien protein and that their dementia is actually a form of mad cow."

Moore's endnotes attribute this to an article by Deborah S. Rogers. But a careful examination of what she actually says reveals that mad cow disease is *one form* of prion disease, a family of fatal ailments spread by a mutant form of protein that has the capacity to convert and kill other proteins (such as your brain). Rogers contends that we shouldn't focus on mad cow disease when *other* prion diseases, such as Creutzfeldt-Jakob disease (CJD), are already known here. Her figure of 200,000 referred to CJD, not to mad cow. Before we're accused of splitting hairs, though, it's more than a technical distinction: Mad cow disease can be spread by eating infected beef, but how CJD is spread, other than by contaminated transplant tissue and other surgical transmission, is unknown.

We'd be tempted to say that Moore stopped reading at the article's title. Actually, he must not have gotten that far. The title is "Mad Cow Here? It's the Wrong Question."

While we're at it, it's worth mentioning that Moore gives some paradoxical advice. He notes that burning does not destroy mad cow disease prions: "But when you burn them, the threat doesn't disappear; *you can't kill them, as I said.* The smoke and ash just carry them to another location. . . ." But, then, he goes on to advise: "Make sure, if you have to eat a burger or steak, to cook that sucker until it's black." Moore is wrong on both counts. Burning *does* destroy prions, cooking does not, so his cooking advisory is not well-taken. They're protein, and cooked meat is still protein, but meat smoke is not. The truth, as usual, is something Moore serves medium rarely.

BUSH'S CAMPAIGN FINANCES: $125 MILLION FROM 700 PEOPLE, DESPITE CAMPAIGN CONTRIBUTION LIMITS

The second chapter of *Stupid White Men* is an open letter to George W. Bush, and in it he refers to "all those dudes who gave you a record-breaking $190 million to run your campaign (two-thirds of which came from just over seven hundred individuals!)" The implication is that most of Bush's presidential campaign was financed by a comparative handful of high rollers, whose contributions averaged more than $170,000 a head.

Hmm . . . Federal elections laws during the 2000 election cycle restricted individual presidential campaign donations to $1,000 each. So exactly how would 700 people contribute about $125 million?

Back to Moore's endnotes. The data he cites actually show that the Republican party has received more than $90 million from 739 contributors in so-called "soft money." *Soft money* donations are made to the GOP as a *party,* not to Bush's campaign fund. Soft money can't be used to explicitly endorse a candidate—the party uses it for voter registration drives, party recruitment, and issue ads that cannot mention a candidate or a race.

And if Moore is making a sharper point here—namely, that Republicans were illicitly using soft-money gains to their candidate's advantage—it's important to note that the Democratic Party is no slouch at raising soft money, either. The *Washington Post* reported that in the 2000 presidential race, "Democrats were essentially even with Republicans on the soft money chase, bringing in $243 million to the GOP's $244.4 million."

And, like the GOP, Democrats' soft money came largely from big donors. A quick glance at the New York Senate 2000 committee that used soft money to back Hillary Clinton's Senate race reveals that nearly $300,000 poured in from just seven people, including the insurance executive who is perhaps best known for pulling the strings that landed Monica Lewinsky her White House internship.

COMMENTATOR FRED BARNES DOESN'T KNOW WHAT THE *ILIAD* AND THE *ODYSSEY* ARE

Next, Moore says that he heard conservative television host Fred Barnes say that modern schooling was so weak that many students don't know what the *Iliad* and the *Odyssey* are. Never one to miss a chance to embarrass a public figure, Moore claims he called Barnes the next day, and recounts their conversation: "'Fred,' I said, 'tell me what the *Iliad* and the *Odyssey* are.' He started hemming and hawing: 'Well, they're . . . uh, you know . . . uh, okay, fine, you got me—I don't know what they're about. Happy now?'"

"No, not really," Moore continues, berating Barnes for hawking his purported wisdom to the nation without having any idea what he was talking about.

Now, Barnes is a graduate of the University of Virginia and held a fellowship at Harvard, the type of places that teach the *Iliad* and the *Odyssey* and, sometimes, even mention Aristotle and Shakespeare. But in the Gospel According to Michael, Barnes has never heard of the most basic of the classics. If we believe Moore's account, Barnes pulled the words Iliad and Odyssey out of the air, not knowing whether they were a rock band or a pair of Greek restaurants. It must be true, for Michael has written it.

But when the *New Republic*'s Alan Wolfe tried to check out the story, Barnes replied that "it never happened." He went on to explain, "One, I've never talked to Michael Moore. Two, I have read the *Iliad* and the *Odyssey*. I didn't read them until I got to college, but I did read them."

No doubt that if Moore were asked to provide phone records, he would first become angry and then suggest that in the course of publicly embarrassing somebody, there's always room for comedy . . . or a fabrication.

NADER DID THE DEMOCRATS A FAVOR, SINCE HIS CANDIDACY CAUSED A TIE IN THE SENATE

Moore has caught some flak for backing Ralph Nader, who many believe siphoned enough liberal votes away from the Democrats to make George W. Bush a president and Al Gore a footnote in history.

Rather than admit that he endorsed the candidate who helped bring Bush to office, Moore attempts to spin this one back to his favor: "If you're going to blame Nader for taking votes from Gore in Florida," he writes, "then you must also give credit to Nader for bringing thousands of new voters to the polls who made the difference for Cantwell—thus allowing the Democrats to force a 50–50 tie in the Senate."

Some favor. At the 2002 mid-term elections, the tie was broken easily, with Republicans retaking both the Senate and the House in landslide victories. Curiously, a letter Moore posted to his web site just the day before the election disappeared shortly thereafter, perhaps because the letter contained Moore's prediction that the Democrats were about to score big.

IN 2001, THE UNITED STATES SPENT A QUARTER-TRILLION DOLLARS ON ONE MODEL OF AIRPLANE

In Chapter 8, Moore attempts to feed his readers another unbelievably outrageous whopper. He claims that in 2001, the Pentagon planned to spend $250 billion on the production of 2800 Joint Strike Fighter planes. Then he goes on to say that the $250 billion ". . . is more than enough to pay the tuition of every college student in America."

Though the average reader likely glossed over that claim, Ben Fritz of Spinsanity.com thought the figure rather strange, since the entire Department of Defense 2001 budget was barely $300 billion. Moore's math would mean that five-sixths of the budget went for building one model of fighter. Fritz checked the sources Moore cited, and found that "[Moore] refers to the Web site of the peace activist group Council for a Livable World (CLW). CLW's own analysis of the 2001 budget, however, shows that $250 billion is the total multiyear cost of the Joint Strike Fighter program, not the amount spent in one year."

So much, we might say, for Moore's credibility as a researcher.

MOORE'S PREDICTIVE ABILITIES

We've learned how Moore fared in his predictions of the 2002 midterm elections. Now let's see how some of his other high-profile predictions measure up:

- **Kim Jong Il of North Korea is really okay and about to straighten out.** Moore notes that North Korean leader Kim Jong Il ". . . has a huge army, and is even suspected of having an atomic bomb. In the past two years, though, Kim Jong Il has begun showing signs of a change of heart, signs that he's emerging from the shadows."

  In reality, Kim Jong Il has been steadily refining plutonium in his quest to make North Korea the first mental ward with nuclear capabilities. In April 2004, the dictator's state news agency stated that the United States and North Korea are "on the brink of nuclear war."

- **. . . And Halliburton!** In that same chapter, Moore predicts big gains for Halliburton stock: "When nominated for the vice presidency, Cheney hemmed and hawed about divesting himself of his Halliburton stock. I guess he knew that good times were still to come."

  On reading this, of course, intelligent readers should have ditched their Halliburton shares. Lo and behold, the value of Halliburton stock promptly fell from $40 to $20 a share.

  Fortunately for Cheney, he divested himself of the stock before the drop. Now the crowd criticizes him for doing it! The *Washington Post* charged that

"the developments at Halliburton since Cheney's departure leave two possibilities: Either the vice president did
not know of the magnitude of problems at the oilfield
services company he ran for five years, or he sold his
shares in August 2000 knowing the company was likely
headed for a fall." (An ironic but unsurprising twist: The
Post had itself been among the media voices arguing
that Cheney had an ethical duty to sell off the stock.)

Okay, so Moore doesn't understand economics, biology,
international relations, or anything else he's writing about.
Let's put the advantage in his court, then, and examine three
areas that he considers serious: the 2000 presidential election, the persecution of his enemies in public education, and
the evils of George W. Bush.

2000 PRESIDENTIAL ELECTION

To Moore, the 2000 presidential election was all just a big conspiracy, long before the legal battle erupted over votes in
Florida. Moore claims that "The coup began long before the
shenanigans on Election Day 2000. In the summer of 1999
Katherine Harris, an Honorary Stupid White Man who was
both George W. Bush's presidential campaign co-chairwoman
and the Florida Secretary of State in charge of elections, paid
$4 million to Database Technologies to go through Florida's
voter rolls and remove anybody 'suspected' of being a former
felon."

Just in case you aren't fully indignant yet, Moore adds
race into the mix: "Harris and Bush knew that removing the
names of ex-felons from the voter rolls would keep thousands
of black citizens out of the voting booth."

As always with Moore, the truth is far more complex, not to mention . . . truthful.

First, some background, which Moore doesn't bother to explain: In 1997, the Miami mayoral race had set something of a local record for voting scandals, due to votes being cast by felons—and some folks who were barred from voting because they were, well, dead at the time.

The *Miami Herald* led the outcry with a Pulitzer Prize–winning investigation, in which it discovered that "more than 100 convicted felons . . . voted in the Miami election last November." Another newspaper reported that "the names of more than 50,000 felons fill the rolls of Florida's registered voters. And the names of nearly 18,000 dead people join them."

The matter stirred the Florida Legislature—not Katherine Harris, as Moore accused—to appropriate $4 million in order to cleanse the voting rosters. According to the *Palm Beach Post*, "State lawmakers decided to weed out felons and other ineligible voters in 1998 after a Miami mayoral election was overturned because votes had been cast by the convicted and the dead."

Moore continues, again shamelessly using the race card for maximum dramatic effect: "31 percent of *all* black men in Florida are prohibited from voting because they have a felony on their record."

Thirty-one percent of black males in Florida have been found guilty of felonies? It's a statistic that should make every reader's jaw drop. By Moore's count that would mean nearly one in three of all African American men in Florida have been found guilty of a felony, and that number sounds absolutely ridiculous.

Back to checking Moore's sources. Perhaps by now, you can guess the outcome. Greg Palast, who was a major critic of the efforts to weed out felons, reported that only about three percent of Florida's African-Americans registered to vote were on the state's purge list.

Moore then cites examples of persons mistakenly identified as felons and thus not permitted to vote. There's little doubt that such mistakes have occurred. In a nation of nearly 300 million, many people share names and dates of birth, and with felons, one has to expect further confusion from their use of aliases. Most of us find one name sufficient, but criminal offenders may use several, so police records include all names used. The important thing to note is that Florida sent notices to voters on the lists, allowing them plenty of time (in most cases, months) in which to contest the claim that they were felons. Proving the success of the initiative, the vast majority of the errors were corrected in time. The *Palm Beach Post* noted that the appellate board heard more than 5,400 appeals and changed over 2,500 determinations, although 108 of those cases could not be determined in time for the election.

Moore goes on to note that convicted felons strongly tend to vote Democratic and then argues that if the mistakenly listed nonfelons had been allowed to vote, they would have given Gore the votes he needed to win.

Logic is not Mike's strong suit. All we know, if he is correct, is that *real* felons vote Democratic. How the vote split for the people whose names were merely confused with those of felons is unknown. Most likely, as with the rest of the country, they would've split almost perfectly between Gore and Bush.

But wait—the pesky *Miami Herald* is back with another election study, and again the results don't exactly favor Moore either. The study found that some predominantly

Democratic counties ignored the lists entirely and let everyone—including felons—vote anyway, with which Moore presumably takes no issue. According to the survey, a sample of just two Florida counties revealed that "At least 39 felons—mostly Democrats—illegally cast absentee ballots . . . if felons cast illegal votes in the same percentages at the polls it could amount to more than 470 illegal ballots locally and more than 2,000 statewide."

At least two thousand illegal votes. This is quite a bit larger than the figure Moore uses to skew the election against Bush and certainly more than enough to give the election fully, and finally, to the man Moore still has not accepted as the winner.

PUBLIC EDUCATION

The irony gets a bit thick when Moore turns to the subject of education. As a good liberal, he must support public education, yet as a critic arguing that Americans are ill-educated morons, he must maintain it is a failure. Mark Twain once remarked that sacred cows make the best hamburger. Moore's problem is that he wants to have his cow and eat it, too.

First he lights into public education, charging that "high school is, we all know, some kind of sick, sadistic punishment of kids by adults," not to mention a "sort of totalitarian dictatorship."

However, Moore believes that *anyone else* who criticizes public education is far out of line. "Considering the face slapping that society gives our teachers on a daily basis," Moore argues, "is it any wonder that so few choose the profession?"

Moore himself didn't settle for a mere face slapping; he went after his teachers with a vengeance. His main target was his own high school principal who, he tells us, ". . . used to let me and my friends skate and play hockey on this little pond beside his house. He was kind and generous . . . Years later, I was asked to play bass in a band that was forming, but I didn't own a bass. He let me borrow his son's."

But in high school, Moore and the principal clashed, and Moore saw no sense in letting decency stand in the way of a good vendetta. Moore's first foray into politics consisted of getting elected to the school board, at age 18, on a platform of firing the principal and his assistant. Moore won the election, and he wastes no time bragging about his victory: "I won, getting the vote of every single stoner between the ages of eighteen and twenty-five (who, though many would probably never vote again, relished the thought of sending their high school wardens to the gallows)."

As to what he accomplished after election, Moore gets a bit ambiguous. He notes that the principal and vice principal resigned, and the principal died of a heart attack; the reader is left to assume that Moore had enough clout with the school board to force them out. Actually, it seems doubtful that Moore had any vote but his own. Don Hammond of Davison told the *Detroit Free Press* that, "He once sat on the board's meeting table, took off his shoes and socks and picked at his toes." Hammond added that Moore had walked out of another board meeting, proclaiming, "I don't want to sit around with you bums." So much for his devotion to public education.

On the next page Moore is back to his preaching: "You would think society's attitude would be something like this:

'Teachers, thank you for devoting your life to my child. Is there ANYTHING I can do to help? I am here for you. Why? Because you are helping my child—MY BABY—learn and grow. . . .'"

A few pages later, though, he forgets his own advice (perhaps because it is meant for others, not himself). He advises students to "Threaten lawsuits—school administrators HATE to hear that word. Just remember, there's no greater satisfaction than seeing the look on the principal's face when you have the upper hand. Use it."

While Moore appears to be somewhat sympathetic to the individual teachers, his attitude about the public education system seems to be "see you in court!"

GEORGE W. BUSH

With Moore, everything is personal; there are no great issues, just foolish, cold-hearted men who refuse to agree with him. Thus, it is inevitable that *Stupid White Men* sets its sights on George W. Bush. Moore lists the President's transgressions, and a mighty list it is.

"He started a new Cold War, this time with China, over an American spy plane that knocked one of their planes out of the sky, killing the pilot."

Ah, yes. The incident where a Chinese fighter pilot (appropriately named Wong Wei) became too aggressive while buzzing a radar reconnaissance plane and managed to collide with it. China's story was that America's lumbering, twin-engine radar aircraft had somehow outmaneuvered and chased down the far faster and more nimble Chinese fighter jet—a piece of propaganda even Stalin-era Soviets would have blushed to write. But for Mike, who never met a leftist totalitarian he didn't like, it must be the truth. Oh, and the "Cold War" that Moore says President Bush reinitiated—the reinitiation consisted of the U.S. objection to China's holding the crew as hostages.

> **"He threatened to unilaterally reduce our presence in the former Yugoslavia, resulting in renewed violence between the ethnic groups in the region."**

Mike has trouble keeping his position straight. In *Bowling for Columbine,* he criticized our bombing in Kosovo—which quickly led to peace between the ethnic groups or at least a dramatic reduction of genocide. In every other context, he objects to American military presence anywhere. Moore complains that the United States uses military force to intervene in local disputes. Here, he's complaining that President Bush threatened to pull our military *out* of a foreign conflict.

> **"He defied UN human rights agreements, resulting in the United Nations removing the United States from its Human Rights Committee."**

Yep. This is the same United Nations that last year chose Libya to chair the committee, either demonstrating a Puckish sense of humor or (more likely) showing just what happens when you let the patients run the asylum. Speaking of which. . .

> **"He cut off any hope of reducing tensions with North Korea, guaranteeing not only that mass starvation there will continue, but that its leader, film nut Kim**

Jong Il, will never return his overdue videos to Block-buster."

It's hard to reduce tensions when a basket case announces he's refining bomb-grade plutonium with the aim of becoming a nuclear power. We might just wonder why North Korea suffers from mass starvation and South Korea is doing rather well. Might Kim Jong Il have some slight role in this?

Moore's vitriol toward George Bush is inevitable; so is the theme of *Stupid White Men*'s closing chapter. Michael Moore, of course. To be specific, Moore on his backing of Ralph Nader, whose candidacy is widely felt to have elected one George W. Bush. Moore's mea culpa comes in the form of a claim that he reversed himself in Florida at the last minute. In a speech given at the University of Florida on October 23, 2000, he told Nader backers to "think long and hard about it" and that "if it's more important for you to stop Bush, you might have to vote for Gore." That night, Moore wrote on his web site, "the story went out that one of Ralph Nader's 'celebrity backers' had given the green light to vote for Gore. . ."

Very strange, since Mike's letter to his followers only three days before (and in which he informed them of the upcoming Florida speech) had been a long diatribe against Gore's running mate, Senator Joe Lieberman, in which he had called the Democrats "wimps and whiners and cry-babies" and argued that "if you vote for Gore-Lieberman, you are voting for two men who don't even believe in their own election! What does that tell us about the other things they SAY they believe in?"

But might Moore have had a sudden change of heart? After Moore repeated the story on Air America, blogger Steven I. Weiss set out to track it down. A Nexis search turned up exactly one story on Moore's speech—so much for word going around the State. The story suggested that Moore had remained an unrepentant Green: He had argued that Bush and Gore were the same, that refusing to vote for Nader because he couldn't win was choosing a president as the "lesser of two evils," and that a majority of voters supported Nader's views. What about the different account Moore gives? Revisionist history, once again.

Stupid White Men took Moore further on the career path begun with *Roger & Me*. Facts no longer mattered, history could be rewritten at will. All that mattered was a rousing rant which demonstrated his (and by reflection, his readers') superiority to others.

SEARCHING FOR TRUTH IN *BOWLING FOR COLUMBINE*

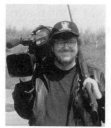

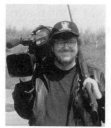

With *Bowling for Columbine,* one of 2002's most widely discussed films, Michael Moore broke into the big time, winning the special jury prize at the Cannes film festival and an Academy Award for Best Documentary Feature.

It's also the most blatant exemplification in Moore's career of how willing he is to subvert the truth in order to support his agenda.

Unfortunately, by the Academy's own definition, *Bowling for Columbine* was not a documentary. Rule 12 of the Academy's official guidelines for selection states that a documentary is a "non-fictional movie." But *Bowling* was largely fiction. The point is not that *Bowling* was biased. No, the point is that *Bowling* was deliberately, seriously, and consistently deceptive. Several statements made in the film are totally misleading. Indeed, even speeches shown on screen were heavily edited, with sentences taken so out of context as to distort the speaker's intended meaning.

In a historical sense, *Bowling* took the documentary back to where it originated, as a postwar application of the tools used in the propaganda films of World War II. In technique,

Bowling may be modern—there's no invisible narrator boom-ing out in the "voice of God" that the Allies will win or the *un-termensch* must be exterminated. But in content, *Bowling* is often as manipulative as totalitarian propaganda.

These are serious charges, we realize, and we will treat them seriously. Let's take the major issues one by one, begin-ning with the film's lengthiest bout with unreality.

THE HESTON OBSESSION

Any examination of the film reveals a deep and perhaps pathological obsession on Moore's part, driven by his appar-ent hatred of the actor Charlton Heston, then president of the National Rifle Association (NRA).

Moore's personal attack on Heston is woven into three separate segments of *Bowling*. In each segment, Moore sum-mons all of his creative powers—which to be fair, are con-siderable—to mislead the viewer into a highly negative view of his target. By the time he's done, he has even managed the considerable feat of portraying Heston—once a leader of the civil rights movement, a personal friend of Martin Luther King, and a regular guest speaker for the Congress of Racial Equality—as a racist.

Moore Lies: Heston and the NRA Marched into Denver, and Defiantly Held a Rally Just a Week after the Columbine Tragedy

A major theme in *Bowling* is that Heston and the NRA are cal-lous toward gun slayings and gun-related violence. In order to make the facts fit into his predetermined thesis, Moore repeat-edly distorts the evidence. *Bowling* begins this claim with a supposed NRA rally held in Denver shortly after the Columbine high school killings in nearby Littleton.

Consider the following sequence in the movie:

First, a shot of weeping children outside Columbine, describing how friends were murdered before their eyes.

Cut to Charlton Heston holding a musket and proclaiming "I have only five words for you: 'from my cold, dead, hands.'"

From there, the film jumps to a shot of a billboard advertising the meeting, while Moore gravely intones, "Just ten days after the Columbine killings, despite the pleas of a community in mourning, Charlton Heston came to Denver and held a large pro-gun rally for the National Rifle Association."

Next, the film cuts to Heston, who appears to be continuing his speech. "I have a message from the Mayor, Mr. Wellington Webb, the Mayor of Denver. He sent me this. It says 'don't come here. We don't want you here.' I say to the Mayor, this is our country, as Americans we're free to travel wherever we want in our broad land. Don't come here? We're already here!"

What conclusions does this sequence lead the audience to draw? As one reviewer put it, "[I]t seemed that Charlton Heston and others rushed to Littleton to hold rallies and demonstrations directly after the tragedy."

This portrayal is, in fact, false.

FACT: Let's put this Denver "large pro-gun rally" in its real context. It was not a pro-gun demonstration called as a response to Columbine, but rather an annual meeting of the members of the NRA, whose place and date had been fixed years in advance.

FACT: Annual meetings of the members of a nonprofit corporation are regulated by law, in the interests of ensuring corporate democracy. Depending on the bylaws, members have the right to debate, pass resolutions, amend bylaws, or choose officers at the meeting. The NRA is a New York corporation, and New York nonprofit corporation law requires an annual meeting of the members.

FACT: The New York statutes *also* rule out the NRA's changing the location or date of the meeting on short notice. To change the time or place, ten days' advance notice had to be given to all voting members. The Columbine tragedy occurred just eleven days before the meeting— and the NRA had 4 million members nationwide who would have had to be notified in the same day's mail.

FACT: At the Denver meeting, the NRA cancelled all events—normally several days of committee meetings, sporting events, dinners, and rallies—all, save the annual members' voting event. "Under its bylaws and New York state law, the NRA must hold an annual meeting," the *Rocky Mountain News* reported, adding, "President Charlton Heston and the group's executive vice president, Wayne LaPierre, said all seminars, workshops, luncheons, exhibits by gun makers and other vendors, and festivities are canceled."

This does cast a slightly different light on what Moore refers to as a "large pro-gun rally." The NRA scaled back their convention in every way they could, maintaining only that which was legally required.

On to Heston's speech, as Moore lets his viewers see it. . . .

Juxtaposed with images of weeping and terrified students, Heston's speech—particularly his "out of my cold, dead hands" cry—seem defiant, scary, and completely detached from the human tragedy of Columbine.

FACT: Heston's "cold, dead hands" speech, which leads off Moore's depiction of the Denver meeting, was not given at Denver after Columbine. It was given *a year later* in Charlotte, North Carolina, and was his gesture of gratitude when given a handmade musket at that annual meeting.

Bowling then continues Heston's speech with his response to the Mayor's request that the NRA not come: The viewer sees pure defiance, plus an angry taunt that the NRA is already there.

FACT: Moore's fabrication here cannot be described by any polite term. It is a lie, a fraud, and a few other things. Carrying it out required a LOT of editing to mislead the viewer. Moore has actually taken audio of seven sentences, from five different parts of the speech, and a section given in a different speech entirely and spliced them together. Each edit is cleverly covered by inserting a still or video footage of the listening audience for a few seconds.

First, right after the weeping victims, Moore puts on Heston's "I have only five words for you . . . cold, dead hands" statement, making it seem directed at them.

Moore then inserts an interlude—a visual of a billboard and his narration. *This is vital.* He can't go directly to Heston's *real* Denver speech. If he did that, you might ask why Heston changed in mid-speech from a purple tie and lavender shirt to a white shirt and red tie, and the background draperies went from maroon to blue. Moore had to separate the two segments with a visual distraction.

Moore's second edit (covered by splicing in a panoramic shot of the crowd) deletes Heston's announcement about scaling back the convention's events. In the actual speech, Heston went on to say, "As you know, we've cancelled the festivities, the fellowship we normally enjoy at our annual gatherings. This decision has perplexed a few and inconvenienced thousands."

Moore then cuts to Heston's response to the Mayor's request: "I said to the Mayor: 'As Americans, we're free to travel wherever we want in our broad land. Don't come here? We're already here!'"

Moore actually puts one edit *right in the middle of the first sentence,* and another at the end! Here's what Heston really said, as a reference to his own World War II vet status: "I said to the mayor, well, my reply to the mayor is, 'I volunteered for the war they wanted me to attend when I was 18 years old. Since then, I've run small errands for my country, from Nigeria to Vietnam. I know many of you here in this room could say the same thing.'"

Moore cuts it after "I said to the mayor" and attaches a sentence from the end of the next paragraph: "As Americans, we're free to travel wherever we want in our broad land." He hides the deletion by cutting to footage of protestors and a photo of the Mayor before going back and showing Heston.

Again, you *think* you are hearing Heston in a continuous audio stream.

Moore then has Heston triumphantly announce, "Don't come here? We're already here!" First, that sentence was clipped from a segment *five paragraphs later* in the speech. Again, Moore uses an editing trick to cover the doctoring, switching to a panoramic shot of the audience as Heston's (edited) voice continues.

What Heston actually said with regard to "We're already here" follows in full. The deleted parts are italicized:

> *NRA members are in City Hall, Fort Carson, NORAD, the Air Force Academy and the Olympic Training Center. And yes, NRA members are surely among the police and fire and SWAT team heroes who risked their lives to rescue the students at Columbine.*
>
> **Don't come here? We're already here.** *This community is our home. Every community in America is our home. We are a 128-year-old fixture of mainstream America. The Second Amendment ethic of lawful, responsible firearm ownership spans the broadest cross section of American life imaginable.*
>
> *So, we have the same right as all other citizens to be here. To help shoulder the grief and share our sorrow and to offer our respectful, reassured voice to the national discourse that has erupted around this tragedy.*
>
> *NRA members are, above all, Americans. That means that whatever our differences, we are respectful of one another and we stand united, especially in adversity.*

Moore's editing has converted a conciliatory, uniting speech into a defiant, divisive one, with each edit so cleverly covered that the audience thinks they've heard the entire Heston presentation!

Moore Lies: Heston and the NRA Marched into Mt. Morris, Michigan, after a Fatal Shooting in That Town

Bowling later juxtaposes another Heston speech with a school shooting of Kayla Rolland at Mt. Morris, Michigan, just north of Flint. Kayla Rolland was a young girl who was shot to death by a fellow elementary school student. Moore makes the claim that "just as he did after the Columbine shooting, Charlton Heston showed up in Flint, to have a big pro-gun rally."

FACT: Heston's speech was given at a "get out the vote" rally in Flint. It was held in October 2000, just before the presidential election. The killing of Kayla Rolland took place in February 2000, eight months earlier.

FACT: George W. Bush and Al Gore were then both in the Flint area, trying to gather votes. Moore himself had been hosting rallies for Green Party candidate Nader in Flint a few weeks before. An article in the *Detroit Free Press* one day after Heston's speech proved this fact: "What do Al Gore, Charlton Heston, Jesse Jackson, Lee Iacocca, and George W., Laura and Barbara Bush all agree upon? That Michigan is a really big deal right now. The candidates, their wives, mothers, and pals are here this week, as postdebate spin control ebbs and political ground control overtakes Michigan with 20 days left to Election Day." The story noted that Heston was in town for the Republicans and Gore himself, along with Jesse Jackson, for the Democrats.

But how does Moore trick the viewer into believing that Heston's election eve appearance was actually a defiant response to a shooting in a nearby town months before?

Moore works by depriving you of context and guiding your mind to fill the vacuum with completely false ideas. And it is brilliantly, if unethically, done. Let's start by deconstructing his method: The entire sequence takes barely forty seconds, and images are flying by so rapidly that you cannot really think about them. Rather, you just form *impressions* of what you see. Moore's goal is to ensure that those impressions are false.

To start the sequence, we see a shot of Moore comforting Kayla's school principal after she discusses Kayla's murder. As they turn away, we hear Heston's voice: "From my cold, dead hands." (Moore again attaches that quote to a moment completely divorced from the context in which it was uttered.)

When Heston becomes visible, he's telling a group that freedom needs you now, more than ever, to come to its defense. The audience's impression: Heston is responding to something urgent, presumably the controversy caused by Kayla's death. And he's speaking about it like a heartless fool. (In reality, Heston's urgent tone reflects the fact that he is part of an election rally, held weeks before the closest presidential election in American history.)

Following that, Moore's voice is heard: "Just as he did after the Columbine shooting, Charlton Heston showed up in Flint, to have a big pro-gun rally."

Moore continues on to say that before he came to Flint, Heston was interviewed by the *Georgetown Hoya* about

Kayla's death. . . . You unconsciously wonder: Why would this be important?

Next, an image of the student newspaper appears on screen, with highlighting on the words of a reporter mentioning Kayla Rolland's name, and further highlighting on Heston's name (not his reply). This image is on screen only a few seconds, which is important.

Ah, you think you spot the relevance: Heston was alerted to the case, and that's why he came to Flint. The newspaper is not on screen long enough for you to notice that Heston is asked about Kayla's case and the Columbine slayings but answers only on the Columbine killings.

And, Moore continues, the case was discussed on Heston's "own NRA" web site. Again, your mind seeks relevance, but Moore will sort it out for you in due time.

Next comes the image of a web site for America's First Freedom (a web site for the NRA, not for Heston) with the text "48 hours after Kayla Rolland was pronounced dead" highlighted and zoomed in on screen—except that the zoom is so fast you cannot read the rest of the page.

As the viewer, your impression becomes clear: Heston did something forty-eight hours after Kayla died. Why else would "his" web site note this event, whatever it is? What would Heston's action have been? It must have been to go to Flint and hold the rally.

In reality, the full sentence posted on the NRA web site actually read: "48-hours after Kayla Rolland is pronounced dead, Bill Clinton is on *The Today Show* telling a sympathetic Katie Couric, 'Maybe this tragic death will help' . . ." It has nothing to do with Heston at all.

Now the scene cuts to protestors, including a woman with a Million Moms March T-shirt, who asks how Heston could come here. She's shocked and appalled as she says, "[I]t's like he's rubbing our face in it."

This caps your impression: She's shocked by Heston coming there, forty-eight hours after the death. Makes sense. He'd hardly be accused of rubbing faces in the tragedy if he came there much later, for a purpose completely unrelated to the death.

The viewer *thinks* he or she understands what transpired—for evidence of that, one need only read a sample of the reviews of *Bowling* during its theatrical release. One reviewer was quick to point out that Heston "held another NRA rally in Flint, Michigan, just 48 hours after a 6 year old shot and killed a classmate in that same town." Another reviewer was more direct in his or her assumptions: "What was Heston thinking going to Colorado and Michigan immediately after the massacres of innocent children?"

Moore's work is brilliant, if evil. Without quite *saying* anything false, he has created in the viewer's mind an entirely false image.

When later interviewed by the *Times of London,* Moore conceded as much. Reporter Clive Davis wrote: "When I spoke to Moore last week, he confirmed Hardy's point about the date of the speech, but angrily denied the allegation that he had misled viewers."

Moore follows with a coup de grâce. Having blackened the character of a man who did nothing to deserve it, Moore sets out to confront Heston in his home and make his truthful responses seem like clumsy lies.

When pressed by Moore's questions, Heston's memory of the Flint event is foggy (he says it was an early morning event and that they then went on to the next rally. In fact the rally was held from 6–7:30 P.M. and was the last event of the day). Heston's lack of recall may reflect the early stages of Alzheimer's, or it may merely be the result of a stressful and hectic schedule—Flint was one rally in a nine-stop tour that covered three States in three days.

Moore asks Heston misleading questions, such as: "After that happened you came to Flint to hold a big rally and, you know, I just, did you feel it was being at all insensitive to the fact that this community had just gone through this tragedy?" Moore continues, "You think you'd like to apologize to the people in Flint for coming and doing that at that time?"

Moore knows the real sequence, and knows that Heston does not. Of course, Heston's unapologetic and somewhat stunned response reflects this. Moore takes full advantage of him . . . and of his viewers.

Moore Paints Heston as a Racist

No, Moore does not directly state that Heston is a racist. But he is the master of creating the false impression to the extent that reviewers came away saying, "Heston looks like an idiot and a racist one at that."

That conclusion stems from Heston's answer when Moore presses him to explain why the United States has more violence than other countries. Heston says that it might be due to the United States "having a more mixed ethnicity" than other nations, as well as Heston's comment that "we had enough problems with civil rights in the beginning." A viewer who accepts Moore's theme that gun ownership is driven by racial fears would naturally conclude that Heston is blaming blacks and the civil rights movement.

FACT: Heston is not talking about race but about racism. In the early 1960s, the civil rights movement was fighting for acceptance. Civil rights workers were being murdered. The Kennedy Administration, trying to hold together a Democratic coalition that ranged from liberals to fire-eater segregationists such as George Wallace and Lester Maddox, found the issue too hot to touch, and offered little support.

Heston got involved. He picketed discriminating restaurants. He worked with Martin Luther King and led the actors' component of King's 1963 march in Washington, which set the stage for key civil rights legislation in 1964.

FACT: Heston personally broke another Hollywood color barrier. In the late 1960s, sixteen states (including Delaware and Indiana) still had laws on the books forbidding interracial marriage, laws that were finally invalidated by a 1967 Supreme Court decision. Even after this, Hollywood had an unwritten rule: no interracial romances. (This led to the ridiculous spectacle of white actresses like Ava Gardner and Yvonne De Carlo playing black women on screen.) Charlton Heston broke that barrier with *Omega Man*. Not one of his better flicks, but in it he as hero and black heroine Rosalind Cash (hand-picked by Heston for that role) wind up kissing—and, the screenplay strongly suggested, sharing a bed as well.

FACT: If Moore wanted to pick a target at which to fling a charge of racism, Heston is about the last fellow he should have chosen. Most of Moore's viewers were born long after the events Heston is recalling. To them, the civil rights struggle consists of sound bytes of Martin

Luther King speaking, people singing "We Shall Overcome," and everyone coming to their senses. Heston, on
the other hand, remembers what it was really like. Lots of
people died. It was a time of strife and violence, despite
the ultimately positive results and despite how worth-
while the struggle. Heston's statement reflects his memory of this.

FACT: Heston fails to explain this properly in *Bowling*,
but we've got to note that Moore (despite his claim that he
left the interview almost unedited) cut a lot of the interview out. Watch closely and you'll see a clock on the wall
near Moore's head. When it's first seen, the time is about
5:47. When Heston finally walks out, it reads about 6:10.
That's twenty-three minutes. We clocked the Heston interview in *Bowling* at five and a quarter minutes. Given
Moore's track record, we'd say the odds are good that Heston's fuller explanation was neatly trimmed out.

Heston's Departure—More Doctored Footage

Realizing that this supposedly friendly interview has turned
into a video bushwhacking, Heston says the interview is over
and leaves the room. Moore and the camera crew follow him,
arriving at the top of a flight of stairs as Heston is below, walking away. Moore asks Heston to stop, Heston turns, and Moore
holds up the photo of the deceased girl Kayla, and plaintively
asks Heston to look at Kayla's photo. Heston continues away. It
is Moore's crowning moment in his character assassination.

And when you look at it carefully, it, too, is almost certainly falsified. The entire sequence is only eighteen seconds
long. The camera angle shifts from Moore's back (showing
Heston walking away) to Moore's front (showing him holding

the picture) to his back to his front to his back again—five perspectives, four changes in camera—all in eighteen seconds.

How did he film that? It seems there are only two ways. With two cameramen, he could post one in front and one behind. Of course, that would be hard to arrange in the few seconds he has available (he and his crew are pursuing Heston and have finally caught up) but it is at least a possibility—until you consider the camera angles.

When we freeze-framed the sequence, it became apparent that two cameramen would have filmed each other as well as Moore. The front footage is taken from a point about level with his chest and clearly shows the area of his left side and shoulder. The back footage is taken from a point immediately off his left shoulder—indeed, his arm and shoulder are visible in it—and it shows the area in front of him down to within a foot of the steps themselves. The front cameraman would have filmed the back camera at Moore's left side, and the back cameraman would have caught the front camera, right in the middle of its image. With five changes in eighteen seconds and no break in the footage, there's no way for two cameramen to have ducked up and down.

So how did he get that footage? There is but one logical conclusion. It was a one-camera shot, and they used a technique well known to news videographers. First, you film from behind, getting Heston departing. Then the cameraman comes around to the front and films Moore holding up Kayla's photo and talking to Heston. In the editing room, the two pieces of footage are spliced together to create an impression that the event was filmed from two angles.

The technique is acceptable in news interviews, because they tend to be almost entirely focused on the interview—and because most serious journalists can be trusted not to misrepresent the content of their interviews. In the case of Moore's "interview" with Heston, on the other hand, it means that what you *thought* you saw, Moore speaking to Heston, was actually filmed *after Heston left*. Moore is standing a good thirty feet from Heston; Heston is facing the other way and walking fast. Yet, simply by saying "Mr. Heston," in a conversational tone of voice, he gets Heston to stop and turn around. Unless Heston has extremely good hearing (which is practically unknown in shooting enthusiasts of his age—until the 1970s, it was thought wimpy to use hearing protection, so older shooters all tend to be deaf as posts), it's probable that Moore was a lot louder and perhaps ruder than what is heard on the tape.

At least at the end of the confrontation, we know whom Moore holds blameworthy for Kayla's death. Not the person who shot her, not the crack-dealing uncle from whom he got the gun, but Charlton Heston.

MYRIAD DECEPTIONS

To be sure, Heston is not the only victim of *Bowling*.

We'll take each of the further deceptions one by one, beginning at the start of the film.

Starting Off with a Bang

In a dramatic scene that sets the kinetic tone for the whole film, Moore begins *Bowling* by going to a Michigan bank that offers Weatherby rifles and shotguns (in place of interest) for certificates of deposit. He then plunks down $1,000 for a twenty-year CD and walks out with the rifle over his shoulder.

Though some have doubts, it's entirely possible that Moore did walk out with the rifle—after all, the bank is a licensed federal firearms dealer and, after filling out paperwork and running an FBI check on him, could legally transfer the rifle to him just as if he had made the purchase at a traditional gun shop.

But there is more to the matter. The bank is in Michigan. At the time of the filming, Moore was a New York City resident—he'd moved there by June 1997.

The significance? The Gun Control Act of 1968 tightly restricts gun transfers between residents of different States. A licensed dealer can transfer a rifle or shotgun to a nonresident, but only if "the sale, delivery, and receipt fully comply with the legal conditions of sale in both such States." This requirement is well known to firearm dealers, and violation is a felony, so they're serious about it. The buyer is also required to produce picture ID to establish his residence, and all that is recorded on the paperwork, which federal agents periodically audit.

New York City has some of the strictest gun laws in the nation. One of them makes it illegal to transfer a rifle or shotgun to anyone who does not hold a rifle and shotgun purchase permit. The permit is supposed to be issued within sixty days of application, although in practice it takes much longer, three to six months being typical.

Something is missing here. At the time, Moore's primary residence was in the state of New York. He either had to spend three to six months before filming the scene to get the necessary permit, which he denies doing, or he had to demonstrate to the satisfaction of the bank that he was a Michigan resident. The film does not make clear how he accomplished this.

Obviously, Moore needed a great opening scene to wow his audience and to ensure they were predisposed to swallow his remaining arguments. Here again he creates a compelling vignette on film by leaving out the explanation of a critical detail.

Michael Moore Caught—Then Lies Again

To illustrate the racist tendencies of politicians (and especially Republican politicians), *Bowling* shows what purports to be a television ad run by George Bush Sr. in his 1988 presidential campaign against Massachusetts Governor Michael Dukakis. At the time, Massachusetts had a "prison furlough" program where prisoners could be given short releases from the clink. As to be expected, some of the prisoners found the outside a preferable place to their cells and never came back.

The Massachusetts legislature thought a modest limit on furloughs might be appropriate, given the failure of the program, and passed a bill forbidding furloughs for inmates with "life without parole" sentences for murder. Governor Dukakis vetoed the legislation, and under his administration, murderers continued to get weekends off with the boys.

Unfortunately for Dukakis, one of them was Willie Horton. Horton, in prison for a brutal stabbing murder, got a furlough, never returned, and then attacked a couple, assaulting both and raping the woman. As might be expected, Horton's furlough and crime spree became an issue when Dukakis ran for president, and the Bush campaign ran a television ad arguing that Dukakis had created a "revolving door" for violent criminals.

Moore wanted to depict the Horton campaign ad as proof of racism, particularly the racism of Republicans—you see, Horton was black. Moore had a problem, though. The Bush ad never mentioned Horton's race, did not show a picture of Horton, and didn't even mention him by name.

Moore solves the problem with a bit of editing. In *Bowling,* the Horton ad begins with a "revolving door" of justice, progresses to a picture of Willie Horton, and ends with dramatic subtitle: "Willie Horton released. Then kills again." Then it ends with the required note that it was paid for by the Bush-Quayle presidential campaign. Moore then intones, "[W]hether you're a psychotic killer or running for president of the United States, the one thing you can always count on is white America's fear of the black man."

FACT: In *Bowling,* Moore spliced together *two different* election ads. He took the revolving door scene and the "paid for by Bush-Quayle" from Bush's real ad. Into that he spliced an ad run by an independent campaign committee, the National Security Political Action Committee, which named Horton and showed his picture in a separate ad. Moore then topped his editing by adding the subtitle "Willie Horton released. Then kills again." There is nothing to reveal that most of the ad just seen was not the Bush-Quayle ad.

This fabrication was caught soon after *Bowling*'s theater release. On Spinsanity.com, Ben Fritz outlined the edit and also noted the most telling slip-up of the scene: Moore apparently didn't even bother to research the events before doctoring the ads to fit his conclusion. In reality, Horton did not "kill again"—his offenses were aggravated assault and rape.

Caught red-handed, Moore (or his distribution partners at Warner Bros.) had the apparent decency to remove the misleading footage from the movie's later release in VHS.

Unfortunately, the footage mysteriously reappeared in the film when *Bowling* was released on DVD.

For the DVD release, Moore did make one minor change, however. He switched his edited-in caption to "Willie Horton released. Then rapes a woman." Obviously Moore had been informed of the Spinsanity.com criticism . . . and responded only by correcting his typo in the inserted caption.

Moore later attempted to defend his veracity via his web site, where he posted a letter addressed to his "Wacko Attackos." About 90 percent of it is devoted to responding to a few easily rebutted criticisms. But when he turns to the Horton ad, Moore is forced to make what must be a painful confession: "Actually, I have found one typo in the theatrical release of the film," Moore writes on his web site. "It was a caption that read, 'Willie Horton released by Dukakis and kills again.'" In fact, Willie Horton was a convicted murderer who, after escaping from furlough, raped a woman and stabbed her fiancé, but didn't kill him. The caption has been permanently corrected on the DVD and home video version of the film and replaced with, "Willie Horton released. Then rapes a woman."

It is difficult to interpret this defense as anything but an admission that the ad's caption was inserted by Moore—and that he was fully aware of the other doctoring and has no intention of changing the footage to let his viewers see the real ad.

No Sense Searching for Cause and Effect

Bowling depicts the juvenile who killed Kayla Rolland as a sympathetic youngster from a struggling family, who just found a gun in his uncle's house and took it to school. As Moore would have you believe, "No one knew why the little boy wanted to shoot the little girl." The closest Moore comes to assigning blame is to link the murder with the fact that the boy's family was struggling because his mother was forced to return to work. Ultimately, Moore points a finger at the sweeping welfare reform bill passed in 1996.

FACT: It had been previously reported that the little boy who killed Kayla had already been suspended from school for stabbing another student with a pencil. What's more, other reports showed the boy had fought with Kayla the day before. Moore himself acknowledges that since the incident, the boy has stabbed another child with a knife.

On to Moore's implication that the causes for the shooting are somehow directly related to a larger, vague social theory. While the exact cause is likely a far more complex answer than Moore has time for, we can draw some basic conclusions from the facts we have about the child's life.

For starters, the boy found the gun he used in the killing at his uncle's place of business—which just happened to be the neighborhood crack house. As David Kopel disclosed in the *National Review,* the gun in question was stolen and purchased by the uncle in exchange for drugs, while the boy's father was already serving a prison term for theft and drug offenses. A few weeks later, police busted the shooter's grandmother and aunt for narcotics sales. And after police hauled the family away, the neighbors applauded the officers. The child's father—whom one might consider a reliable source concerning his son—offered a possible theory to a reporter, who filed the tragic report: "His son seemed angry, according to Owens. He doesn't know why, but he suspects that his son may be reacting to his absence. Owens was sent to jail when his son was 2 years old."

A CBS News report offered another theory, by way of a policeman working the case: "The day the boy was born he went from hospital to crack house," says one investigator. "He never had a chance."

The reality of the crime was simple. Kayla Rolland was killed by an angry, violent kid, who had been born into a family in which violence was expected and lawbreaking normal. In this setting, Moore chooses to portray the killer, and the mother who raised him in that environment as victims, unable to elevate their lives above the circumstances they'd been dealt.

Making a Missile out of a Molehill or, in This Case, a Satellite

Bowling contains a sequence filmed at a Lockheed Martin manufacturing facility near Columbine. Moore begins by saying that no one knows why the Columbine killers decided to strike. He then notes that the community is home to Lockheed Martin, our largest defense contractor. Moore intones that the missiles with their "Pentagon payloads" are trucked through the town "in the middle of the night while the children are asleep." Moore asks the company representative, Evan McCollum, whether knowledge that weapons of "mass destruction" were being built nearby might have motivated the Columbine shooters: "So you don't think our kids say to themselves, 'Dad goes off to the factory every day, he builds missiles of mass destruction. What's the difference between that mass destruction and the mass destruction over at Columbine High School?'"

FACT: After *Bowling* was released it was revealed that the Lockheed Martin plant does not build weapons-type missiles; it makes rockets for launching satellites. Ironically, one of its projects is the ultimate in beating swords into plowshares: the conversion of old Titan II missiles, originally built for launching nukes in the 1970s, into satellite carriers.

Moore's "Wacko Attackos" letter gave his response to these facts, but his rebuttals were weak at best. "[T]he Lockheed rockets now take satellites into outer space," Moore wrote. ". . . some are top secret Pentagon projects (like the ones that are launched as spy satellites and others which are used to direct the launching of the nuclear missiles should the USA ever decide to use them)."

Not much of a defense of his veracity. Although we can probably see why he *didn't* want to say: "Dad goes off to the factory every day, he builds spy satellites. What's the difference between spy satellites and the mass destruction over at Columbine High School?'"

Investigating the discrepancy, the *Times of London* found that McCollum insisted that Moore had not made an honest mistake. The issue had come up during the filmed interview, and "when Moore mentioned weapons, McCollum says he made it clear to him that the plant did not build any."

Moore Fails American History 101

In a cartoon history tale, with the narrator talking rapidly, *Bowling* equates the NRA with the Klu Klux Klan, observing that the NRA was founded in 1871, "the same year that the Klan became an illegal terrorist organization." *Bowling* goes on to depict Klansmen doffing hoods to become the NRA, and an NRA character helping to light a burning cross while another helps lynch a black.

This scene is Moore at his lowest—which is about as low as it can get. Moore's implications are diametrically opposed to the truth.

FACT: The NRA was founded in 1871 by act of the New York Legislature, at the request of former Union officers, General George Wingate, who had commanded a company in the 22nd New York Volunteers, and Colonel William Church, who had been a staff officer in a New York Brigade. Both were then National Guard officers, and both had been appalled by the poor level of marksmanship their men, largely urban New Yorkers, had shown during the Civil War.

FACT: The Klan was founded in 1866, not 1871, and quickly became a terrorist organization. In 1871, recognizing the dangers posed by the Klan, President Ulysses S. Grant signed into law the federal Ku Klux Klan Act and the Enforcement Act. These criminalized interference with civil rights, and empowered the president to use troops to suppress the Klan. That Grant signed these measures into law the same year that the NRA was founded proves nothing, of course. Grant used these provisions vigorously, suspending habeas corpus and deploying troops. Under his leadership more than five thousand arrests were made and the Klan was dealt a serious (if all too short-lived) blow.

FACT: Grant's vigor in disrupting the Klan earned him unpopularity among many racist whites, but Frederick Douglass praised him, and an associate of Douglass wrote that African Americans "will ever cherish a grateful remembrance of his name, fame and great services."

FACT: After Grant left the White House, the NRA elected him as its eighth president. He succeeded General Winfield Scott Hancock, hero of Gettysburg.

FACT: After Grant's term, the NRA elected General Philip Sheridan, who used his power as military commander of the Union forces occupying the region to remove the governors of Texas and Louisiana from office for failure to suppress the Klan.

FACT: The affinity of the NRA for enemies of the Klan is hardly surprising. The NRA was founded by former Union officers, and eight of its first ten presidents were Union veterans.

FACT: During the 1950s and 1960s, groups of blacks organized as NRA chapters in order to obtain surplus military rifles to fight off Klansmen. (One, Robert F. Williams, wrote a book about it, *Negroes with Guns,* after his rifle club shot up a Klan attack on his house. He served both as a chapter chairman of NAACP and as president of his gun club.)

In short, it is hard to conceive of two more diametrically opposed organizations than the NRA and the Klan. Moore's slander is on a par with claiming the Veterans of Foreign Wars is a Nazi fan club.

Moore Comes to the Aid of the Taliban

In discussing military assistance to various countries, *Bowling* asserts that the United States gave $245 million in aid to Taliban-ruled Afghanistan in 2000 and 2001.

FACT: The aid in question was *humanitarian* assistance, given through U.N. and nongovernmental organizations, to relieve famine in Afghanistan. Various numbers are given for the amount of the aid, and some say several million went for clearing landmines, a use that Moore might be expected to approve (even if they were Soviet-issue landmines).

Gunning for a Point

In one scene, Moore uses brief flashes of international gun homicide statistics, measured in raw numbers. (Raw numbers stack the odds, of course: Australia has but one-fourteenth the population of the United States, Germany under a third, and Canada an eighth.)

The United States comes off badly in the comparison, racking up 11,127, compared to a few hundreds in the other selected nations. How Moore got to 11,127 was not entirely clear when *Bowling* was released: He didn't cite the particular year to which the figures supposedly applied, and the FBI, in 1999–2001, was only reporting about 8,000 gun homicides per annum. Moore subsequently named his source: the Center for Disease Control's National Center for Health Statistics' figures for 1999. One minor problem: their 1999 figures amount to 11,127 only if you include the numbers for police shootings of perpetrators and uses of firearms in self-defense.

Moore is hand-picking his statistics as well. International comparisons lead to some interesting results. In terms of homicide rates worldwide, the United States comes in at an unimpressive twenty-third place. It only made the list by edging out Armenia and Bulgaria. Its long time rival as a superpower, the states of the former Soviet Union, absolutely flatten the United States in head-to-head competition: Russia has *four times* the U.S. murder rate. Ukraine and Estonia, two former Soviet Republics, have twice its rate. Even Poland ranks higher. And South Africa's showing is *ten times* the U.S. rate!

Let's look at another violent crime: rape. Using the measurement of number of rapes per 1,000 population, the United States ranks ninth, at .32, just ahead of Iceland. Canada is fifth, at .75, over double the U.S. rate, and Australia is third with .80. The United States certainly comes off as a much safer place for women. One reason might be that American women pack iron. When in 1995 Professors Gary Kleck and Marc Gertz undertook the most extensive study to date of firearm self-defense (including polling of almost 5,000 persons), they got some astonishing answers. First, Americans used firearms for self-defense in over 2 million cases a year. Second, women and minorities were represented disproportionately among defensive users.

Of course, Moore does conclude that firearms ownership is not the problem, pointing to the example of the Canadians. He could have done better by referring to Switzerland, long hailed as a nation of riflemen. As the BBC reported, the 6 million Swiss civilians own about 2 million guns, and about 600,000 fully automatic rifles (machine guns in the common parlance). More than 200,000 attend annual marksmanship competitions. Despite this, "[V]iolent crime is extremely rare. There are only minimal controls at public buildings and politicians rarely have police protection."

The Swiss system worked rather well in past years: World War II Nazi planners, projecting 200,000 casualties in the event of a Swiss invasion, decided to leave the Swiss alone. Switzerland, in 2000, had a whopping total of 69 homicides, and a homicide rate under 1 per 100,000, a rate lower than France, Germany, the United Kingdom, Norway, and Denmark.

The Case of the Mysterious B-52 Plaque

Bowling shows footage of a B-52 on display at the Air Force Academy, while Moore scornfully intones that the plaque underneath it "proudly proclaims that the plane killed Vietnamese people on Christmas Eve of 1972."

The plaque actually reads that "Flying out of U Tapo Royal Thai Naval Airfield in southeast Thailand, the crew of 'Diamond Lil' shot down a MIG northeast of Hanoi during 'Linebacker II' action on Christmas eve 1972." The point being that downing a fighter was one rare event. The B-52 had little defensive weaponry: no missiles and only a single gun, in the tail. (A World War II B-17 packed anywhere from ten to fifteen guns in seven positions.) If an enemy fighter got through its escort screen, the B-52 usually went down. Diamond Lil managed to survive.

Now that Moore has brought out *Bowling* in DVD format, we can watch him spinning the tale even farther. In the add-on disk, Moore lectures to a university crowd, "And they've got a plaque on there proudly proclaiming that this bomber, this B-52, killed thousands upon thousands of Vietnamese—innocent civilians." Well, these casualties are entirely possible (it was a *bomber*, after all)—the discrepancy is that the plaque doesn't refer to this in the slightest.

A Dog and Gun Show

Moore narrates the story of a lamebrained deer hunter who thought it would be amusing to have a photo of his dog with his hunting rifle slung across its back. The hunter put his rifle on his dog's back with a sling around its neck, and tried to photograph the scene. The gun discharged, hitting the hunter in the leg. As Moore relates the story, you see a sad-looking dog with a rifle on its back, shoulder strap around its neck, whimpering at a prostrate man.

Of course, what we're seeing is neither the actual dog nor the actual man—but Moore never explains that you're looking at a reenactment, as most responsible filmmakers would. The recoil from the rifle would have lifted the dog into the next zip code. Not to mention, the cameraman would hopefully show some concern about first aid rather than continuing to film. In actuality, the Darwin Award contender had a still camera, not a video, as Mike Pesea of NPR confirmed by interviewing Michigan officials.

The Vain Search for Substance

Bowling probably has a good point when it suggests that the media feeds off fear in a search for the fast buck.

Bowling cites some examples: the razor-blades-in-Halloween-apples scare, the flesh-eating bacteria scare, and more. The examples are taken straight from Barry Glassner's excellent book on the subject, *The Culture of Fear,* and Moore interviews Glassner on camera for the point.

Then Moore does exactly what he condemns in the media. He takes two horrendous tragedies and turns them into evidence of a growing epidemic.

Given the prominence of schoolyard killings as a theme in *Bowling for Columbine,* it's hard to believe that (while asking him about other fears and menaces) Moore failed to ask Glassner about schoolyard homicides. If Moore did get such footage, it was left on the cutting room floor. After all, Glassner counts rampant schoolyard shootings among the mythical fears of our culture, pointing out that three times as many Americans are killed by lightning as die in school shootings. While the rarity of such killings eluded Moore in *Bowling for Columbine* (where such a statistic would have interfered with his theme), he makes no secret of Glassner's statistic in *Stupid White Men*, in which he writes: "You're twice as likely to be killed by lightning as by a gunshot in school."

But what of Moore's inference that the media has played a role in escalating gun violence through it's overreporting of isolated events? As one of his interviewees notes, over a period when homicide rates were falling by 20 percent, media coverage of murder increased by 600 percent. While that statistic may be shocking, it's a great example of how one fact can be used to support very different conclusions. Flip it around. When media coverage of homicides increased 600 percent, homicide rates fell by 20 percent. One can more easily argue from Moore's figures that the media coverage of homicides drives the homicide rate *down*. So much for Moore's attempt to pass off his chosen interpretation as the Truth.

We can take this further. During the 1990s, homicide rates in the United States went into their steepest decline in decades, with handgun homicides leading the way. Between 1997 and 2001, firearm homicides fell from 10,729 to 8,719, according to FBI figures. That was the same period that saw the welfare reform laws, the bombing in Serbia, several million firearms sold each year—everything, in short, that Moore tries to blame for violence.

Bowling for Columbine has less documentary value than the average Bugs Bunny cartoon. You see Heston giving a speech—but it's doctored. You see history—but unconnected facts are given a particular Moorewellian spin. You hear that a factory is making weapons of mass destruction—actually, it's building satellite launch platforms. You're led to believe that a rally was a response to a shooting, but it turns out it was eight months later, in anticipation of an election. You watch a Bush-Quayle campaign ad, but in reality it was an ad Moore himself assembled. For Pete's sake, you can't even trust Moore to honestly report the inscription on a monument!

Postwar filmmakers gave us the documentary; Rob Reiner's *Spinal Tap* gave us the mockumentary. Moore succeeds with a new genre, the crockumentary.

Ultimately, Moore's *Bowling for Columbine* is illustrative of what it condemns. Moore argues that the media (1) distorts reality and (2) hypes fear of other Americans because (3) fear is good for a fast buck. Moore distorts reality, hypes fear of other Americans ("are we a nation of gun nuts, or just nuts?") and, well, made several million fast bucks.

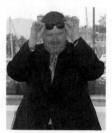

MOORE MONEY

Michael Moore is, as the saying goes, many things to many people. To millions of Americans and Europeans, he is a hero, a valiant crusader, even a prophet.

How does a man with so many contradictions manage to blind his enormous trove of followers to how hypocritical he really is? How does he get away with it?

First of all, Moore poses as the simple spokesman of the working class.

Of course, he does expect to get paid for it. To the tune of $55 million gross for *Bowling for Columbine* alone. What of it? "Average working stiffs were willing to . . . pay seven bucks to see my movie," Moore commented in a recent interview, "So if they're going to give me their money what am I going to get with it? Get a big boat? I don't think so."

No, not a boat—God forbid one should be so extravagant. Moore penny-pinches instead with a $1.9 million apartment in Manhattan.

When he needs to get away from Manhattan's West Side, there's a cozy $1.2 million summer house on Torch Lake in Michigan—a nice beachfront site. (In fact, there was a bit of trouble when the government discovered he was "improving the beach" by filling in wetlands without a permit.)

According to Moore, he travels simply. "Yes, I have a mini-van. . . . I love this minivan. It's roomy, has a smooth ride, and sits about a foot above the cars in front of me so I can see everything."

Of course, he loosens up the purse strings when he's on the road—which is often. On promotional tours, he's apt to be found traveling by private jet or getting chauffeured in rented SUVs and escorted by bodyguards. When granting interviews in San Francisco for *Bowling,* an unshaven Moore held forth in a ritzy $5,200/day presidential suite.

Still, to hear it from Moore, making money means nothing to him, and it's too bad other Americans aren't like him. As he moaned to the *San Francisco Chronicle* in 2003: "Our ethic is 'Every man for himself. Pull yourself up by your bootstraps. Me, me, me, me, me.'" Or as he told Cornell students the previous year: "'Me, me, me, me.' That's the American way. That's what's got to stop."

Of course, the hard-working man is worthy of his hire. Moore charged Cornell University students $10,000 for that speech.

The price went up as he discovered what the market would bear. The University of Texas had to ante up $25,000. When Kansas University students asked him to speak at their student seminar on grassroots politics, he demanded the students put up $30,000. "According to student body president Andy Knopp, the Student Senate pledged $15,000 for the visit, $5,000 of which was out of the Senate's reserve fund." The balance of the fee came from other campus organizations.

His own greed did not stop him from pontificating on CNN's *Crossfire* in 2002: "I agree with Pope John Paul II when he said that capitalism is a sin. This is an evil system, Bob." Curious then that Moore's former manager, Douglass Urbanski, attested to the *Times of London* that Moore was indeed "money obsessed."

He may care about the victims of Columbine but not to the point of letting it affect his profit. When he offered a special screening of *Bowling for Columbine* to survivors and grieving parents, they were shocked that they were expected to pay admission. "Maybe now that he has made millions of dollars off the blood of our children he could toss a DVD or two our way to view," parent Ann Kechter wrote.

Moore's deepest sympathies are with the American worker, particularly those of General Motors. Even though he has no intention of buying the junk the worker makes. In *Stupid White Men,* he casually writes, "When I became an adult I decided I didn't want a General Motors car—mainly because they broke down more often than I did. So I bought Volkswagens and Hondas and drove around town with pride."

He believes that Americans are obsessed with fear—and yet the propagation of fear seems to top the agenda of *Bowling for Columbine.*

Of course Moore has no use for overseas sweatshops or those who exploit them. "[F]actory workers in China . . . earn 12 cents an hour making those cute toys for Disney," he writes in *Dude, Where's My Country?* But those fine principles waver when there's a deal on the table. When Moore needed six million dollars to produce *Fahrenheit 9/11,* he went right to Disney subsidiary Miramax Films for a hefty chunk of sweatshop money.

He sides with the unions, for sure. Except, of course, when his employees try to unionize against him. According to Eric Zicklin, who worked as an associate producer on Moore's *TV Nation:* "Michael said, 'I'm getting a lot of heat from the union to call you guys writers and pay you under the union rules. I don't have the budget for that. But if they keep coming down on me that'll mean I'll only be able to afford one of you and the other one's gotta go.'"

Moore's public persona is Marx with a haircut and a baseball cap, spouting such rhetoric as "[O]n some level, do you think capitalism is okay? No, not really. . . . When I say that last line in the film, 'One evil empire down, one to go, our system is the one that's got to go.'" But his personal values often seem more in line with Marx's contemporaries, the robber barons:

- Wealth proves personal worth. "I'm a millionaire, I'm a multi-millionaire. I'm filthy rich," Moore boasted on *Fox News,* "You know why I'm a multi-millionaire? 'Cause multi-millions like what I do. That's pretty good, isn't it? There's millions that believe in what I do. Pretty cool, huh?"

- Those who question his wealth are merely jealous failures. "They're just pissed because they're not sitting in this apartment," he told another interviewer, "They played by the rules, and now they're a grunt at *Newsweek* or the *New Yorker* or someplace like that and they want to know why they're living with five other people in a five-floor walk-up . . ."

- What's good for Moore is good for America. "That sort of pious, ascetic griping [about his money] is how the left

lost the mainstream in the eighties, he believes: [I]t became a bunch of whining, dowdy, priggish depressives.
. . . He wants to bring back to the left a sense that pleas-
ure is O.K., that self-indulgence isn't always evil."

Ok, we'll rest our case . . . demonstrating that Moore is
a hypocrite is as challenging as fishing at Sea World. With a
case of dynamite.

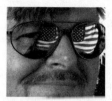

MICHAEL MOORE'S
LAST DAYS IN OFFICE

As Moore himself notes in *Stupid White Men*, our presidents have a curious tradition of enacting a flurry of last-minute executive orders in their final days and weeks in office. Often, these orders are intended to shore up their legacies of good deeds. The soon-to-be-replaced president can also get credit for having done the Right Thing, while sticking his successor with all the cost and trouble of actually having to do it.

Some presidents have imposed regulations designed to help regular folks—measures that would've drawn ire from powerful lobbyists had they not waited until the waning days of their term. Others have taken the opportunity to reward long-standing supporters with grants in an effort to "solidify the base." The rationale seems to be that they'll need to tap gently on the wallets of these folks again when it comes time to build the presidential library.

It got us thinking. Wouldn't it be nice if the roles of dissimulating documentarian and self-aggrandizing author were elected positions—with limited terms? Here would be the wish list of executive orders we'd hope Michael Moore would enact on the way out of his all-too-public office:

- You'd really have to swallow your pride on this first one, Mike, but here goes anyway: Donate $58,000—the same amount *Mother Jones* packed in the U-Haul for you—to the city of Flint, Michigan, in both a symbolic and literal gesture to offer them some retroactive help. Now that you're a multimillionaire resident of New York City, it's the least you could do.

- Speaking of Flint: Apologize to the kind folks of that city, many of whom you embarrassed and denigrated for comedic effect in *Roger & Me*, including some old friends of yours.

- And then there's the folks at Columbine High School. They've been trying to build a memorial to the slain for years but haven't been able to fund it. We don't imagine a certain person who made millions off their tragedy could chip in, oh, just half the cost?

- This one's tough, but fair. Remember that cardboard cutout of Saddam you used to cart around with you to book signings in order to lampoon our Armed Forces for not having located the former Iraqi president? Well, Mike, now that Saddam's in an undisclosed location of our country's choosing, it'd be nice to apologize to those young men and women serving our country and thank them for a job well done. And while you're at it, you also owe an apology to Elian Gonzalez, for smearing his dead mother in a letter on your web site. How about an apology to Wesley Clark for damaging his presidential hopes by starting the unfounded deserter claims about George

W. Bush? Or how about a sit down with the *TV Nation* writers who've documented your unwillingness to pay them?

Phew. That last one turned out to be longer than expected. On second thought, it might be easier on you to take a couple of million and give some unemployed people jobs by opening the Michael Moore Unpresidential Library. You could fill the shelves with a bunch of books that have splashy covers but empty pages, offer viewings of the uncut footage of your films, and recite the unwritten footnotes of your works—for the public to review at their leisure.

Oh, there's just one more item on our wish list, Mike. This one is pretty easy:

GIVE BACK YOUR ILLEGITIMATE OSCAR!

There, that about does it. Just a few humble suggestions. Hey, it's your legacy.

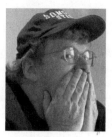

DUDE, WHERE'S YOUR INTEGRITY?

*D*ude, *Where's My Country?* begins, as do all of Michael Moore's works, with himself.

To be precise, he begins with how 9/11 affected him, though he is willing to allow, albeit briefly, that it affected some others, too. As Moore writes in the introduction, "[A] line producer we have worked with, Bill Weems, was not okay. As the networks started to run a scroll along the bottom of the TV with the names of those who were on the planes, along came Bill's name on the screen. . . [h]e was dead and—how do they say it?—'life as we knew it was changed forever.' . . . Things certainly changed for Bill's wife and his seven-year-old daughter."

This marks progress: Moore, the quintessential narcissist, seems to be learning how to *sound* thoughtful and caring.

Or perhaps the emotion here is the product of his editors. While *Dude* was still being put together, Moore got loose from his handlers and gave a very different and more characteristic take on 9/11 during a speaking tour in Britain. British columnist Yasmin Alibhai-Brown, who had taken her son to see Moore perform at the Roundhouse in North London, wrote of his performance: "The U.S. radical and author of the best-selling book *Stupid White Men* was (mostly) clever, funny, angry, sharp, iconoclastic and skeptical. . . ." The speech lost its charm, though, when "Moore went into a rant about how the passengers on the planes on 11 September were scaredy-cats because they were mostly white. If the passengers had included black men, he claimed, those killers, with their puny bodies and unimpressive small knives, would have been crushed by the dudes, who as we all know take no disrespect from anybody."

The "comedy" routine was a poor choice of requiem for his friend Bill Weems and the others who died—some while valiantly fighting to retake their aircraft.

(It's also worth noting that Moore's immediate reaction to the events of 9/11 were unfortunately in character. On September 12, 2001, he quite insensitively suggested that the terrorists killed the wrong people, if their intention was to get back at Bush: "If someone did this to get back at Bush, then they did so by killing thousands of people who DID NOT VOTE for him! Boston, New York, DC, and the planes' destination of California—these were places that voted AGAINST Bush!")

Whatever the cause, Moore's uncharacteristic lapse from egocentricity at the beginning of *Dude* has the lifespan of a neutrino. By page xi of *Dude*'s introduction, he returns to his old form, beginning with three pages of complaints about how 9/11 delayed release of his previous tome, *Stupid White Men*. "The publisher held the books hostage for five long months," says Moore, and then tried to "censor me and the things I wanted to say."

Moore was apparently not impressed by the notion that perhaps it was not advisable, in the wake of September 11,

DUDE, WHERE'S YOUR INTEGRITY?

2001, to release a book that began with a diatribe against the commander in chief, called the United States an "idiot nation" and the secretary of defense "Chicken Little," and had a chapter titled "Kill Whitey." Rather than attempting to understand why the publisher might want to postpone publication, he concluded in typical Moore fashion that the motivation must have been some conspiracy to censor.

SEVEN QUESTIONS, SEVEN ANSWERS

After leading off *Dude* with fourteen pages of Mike's woes, we finally get to Chapter 1, comprised of seven questions directed to George W. Bush.

Although President Bush has yet to reply to Moore (a few trifling presidential duties keeping him busy and all of that), we can imagine the answers he *might* provide to Moore's seven questions.

Question No. 1: Is it true that the bin Ladens have had business relations with you and your family off and on for the past 25 years?

Yeah, and so what? The bin Ladens are one gigantic family. Four wives apiece, remember? When the founder of the clan died in 1988, he left 54 kids (some say 53: He may not have been able to keep track himself). Add in grandkids, in-laws, uncles, aunts, and cousins, and they'd need a convention center to host a family dinner. They're the busiest and one of the wealthiest families in Saudi Arabia, if not the entire Middle East region. And in case you haven't heard, with the exception of Osama (whom they disowned long ago), they lean toward the West and the United States. The very reason they had to be evacuated from the United States was that so many of them had chosen to attend school at American universities.

Besides, Mike, aren't you forgetting your own skepticism about Osama's involvement in 9/11? Might we refer you to your own book, in particular question three, below, where you suggest that Osama is innocent. Why is Osama the *only* bin Laden whom you defend?

Question No. 2: What is the "special relationship" between the Bushes and the Saudi royal family?

A very special one, Mike. In case you haven't heard, Saudi Arabia is the top supplier of oil to the United States, the site of several of our key military bases, and our ally in both Gulf wars. Do you want a president who is on a first-name basis with their international leadership or not? I suppose you'd be happier if *el presidente* was, instead, on a first-name basis with the president of France, you know, Jacques what's his name? Sorry Mike, but we need oil more than we need cheese and canned garden snails.

As you yourself write, "A major chunk of the American economy is built on Saudi money. They have a trillion dollars invested in our stock market and another trillion sitting in our banks. If one day they chose to suddenly remove that money, our corporations and financial institutions would be sent into a tailspin. . . ." All the more reason to have a president who can talk to Prince Bandar of Saudia Arabia as if he were a family member, right?

Oh, yes, you say, they're "among the worst and most brutal dictatorships in the world." But you yourself don't mind dictatorships, do you? You griped when Bush overthrew the

Taliban, which made Saudi Arabia look like an ACLU convention. Ditto when we made Saddam Hussein close up his customized torture parlors. And you treat that lunatic in North Korea (who's starved a million of his own people to death) as a charming eccentric. According to you, Mike, Kim Jong Il is "a *huge* movie buff" who "shares an appreciation of the whimsical world of entertainment with his eldest son." Are you really suggesting that Kim Jong II is less dangerous to the United States because he likes movies?

Question No. 3: Who attacked the United States on September 11—a guy on dialysis from a cave in Afghanistan, or your friends, Saudi Arabia?

Mike, at this point it appears you need help reading your own material. A few pages earlier you made a big fuss about the connections between the Bush family and the bin Laden family, implying that our president had a direct link to the masterminds of the 9/11 disaster. Next, you try to convince us that Osama bin Laden, living in a cave on a non-transportable dialysis machine, would not and could not have been able to organize the plans that resulted in the 9/11 tragedies. See a contradiction here? You can't have it both ways, Mike.

You go on to write that the Saudis were responsible. Here again you get caught up in your own hyperbole. You want to blame the tragedy on the Saudis, but, remember, you've told us that they have a couple of trillion invested in the United States. How much do you think they lost in the wake of 9/11?

You ask: "George, apparently you were a pilot once—how hard is it to hit a five-story building at more than 500 miles an hour?" Mike, you weren't a pilot once, or you'd know.

Since the Wright brothers managed to get off the ground in that badly balanced contraption, we've learned how to build aircraft that are dynamically stable. If you haven't heard the term, that means that so long as they have sufficient power, they put the nose down, they pick up speed, that increases lift, and the nose comes back up. Flying a plane in a straight line isn't, in fact, all that hard. Add in modern control systems and . . . well, there's a pilot's joke that soon the cockpit will be occupied only by the pilot and a trained dog. The job of the dog is to bite the pilot if he tries to touch the controls.

Look, Mike, the most difficult parts of flying are the takeoff and the landing. The hijackers let the real pilots handle the first and didn't have to worry about the second.

Question No. 4: Why did you allow a private Saudi jet to fly around the U.S. in the days after September 11 and pick up members of the bin Laden family and then fly them out of the country without a proper investigation by the FBI?

Mike, it may not have occurred to you, but bin Laden wasn't a very good name to have on your driver's license and credit cards just after September 11. A Saudi was stabbed in Boston; in Arizona, some poor Sikh was killed just because he was seen wearing a turban! If someone had gotten the bright idea to start lynching the innocent end of the family, that would have created a human rights catastrophe and a world-class diplomatic row—right? What's more, it's recently come to light that former White House terrorism expert Richard Clarke (whom you may have noticed, isn't terribly biased in Bush's favor of late) says that no bin Laden left until Clarke himself cleared it with the FBI.

Question No. 5: Why are you protecting the "second amendment rights" of potential terrorists?

Mike's complaint here is that the attorney general said the Brady Act background checks on firearm purchasers could not be used to search for terrorist suspects.

Now, Mike, there is a thing in this country called the rule of law. When Congress passed the Brady Act, it required firearm dealers to call in every firearm sale to a central database system, which would run a criminal record background check on the buyer. The statute included the provision that if the system determined that the buyer was legit, then (quoting here directly from the law), "The system shall . . . destroy all records of the system with respect to the call (other than the identifying number and the date the number was assigned) and all records of the system relating to the person or the transfer."

To be sure, there is ambiguity in the Brady Act about how and when records can be used, but Ashcroft's interpretation was supportable by the language of the act. If you have problems with the Brady Act, Mike, you should direct them to Bill Clinton, who signed the statute into law, or the Brady Campaign, which drafted it.

Mike, you like to pose as a civil libertarian, which means espousing values like the rule of law, limited executive powers, and personal privacy. Yet here you're complaining that Ashcroft *didn't* use his full authority. Your reaction lends weight to the adage: if you want to persuade a conservative to support a bill that betrays his principles, tell him it's an anticrime measure;

if you want to persuade a liberal to do the same, tell him it's directed at gun ownership. (In case you haven't noticed, Mike, the Feds could use the Brady Act to create a national database, not only of criminal records, but of mental health commitments, divorce restraining orders, dishonorable military discharges, and renunciations of American citizenship. The type of database J. Edgar Hoover would have given his eye teeth and best evening gown to control).

Question No. 6: Were you aware that while you were governor of Texas, the Taliban traveled to Texas to meet with your oil and gas company friends?

Let's get this straight, Mike. You're blaming Bush because the Taliban visited Texas while he was governor? When you came up with this doozey, were you aware that representatives of a foreign government don't have to get a governor's permission to come into the country or even into his state?

If the government were to bar suspect foreign leaders from entering the country though, that responsibility would fall with the president. And at the time the president was—you guessed it, there seems to be pattern developing here—a fellow named Bill Clinton. In fact, it was Clinton's own State Department that sponsored the Taliban's second visit to the States.

Again, you've failed to read your own work, Mike. On page 27 of *Dude,* you wrote that "After Texas, the Taliban dictators moseyed on over to Washington, D.C., where they met with Karl Inderfurth, assistant secretary of state. . . . in May 1998, two Taliban members—this time in the U.S. sponsored by Clinton's State Department—took in some more sites. . . ."

Question No. 7: What exactly was that look on your face in the Florida classroom on the morning of September 11 when your chief of staff told you, "America is under attack"?

We can assume safely that Bush's answer would NOT be (1) "the people who died on the plane were a bunch of scaredy-cats" nor (2) "I wish they had targeted a place with more Gore supporters" nor (3) "I hope this won't hold up the release of my book."

Mike, can you say the same?

NEXT, PLEASE

In Chapter 2, "Home of the Whopper," Moore plays on the theme that George W. Bush must have been intentionally lying when he and his officials said Hussein had weapons of mass destruction. If so, we can only observe, Bush had good company. After all, it was—yet again—President Bill Clinton who, in February 1998, told the Joint Chiefs of Staff that ". . . [t]he community of nations may see more and more of the very kind of threat Iraq poses now: a rogue state with weapons of mass destruction, ready to use them or provide them to terrorists. If we fail to respond today, Saddam and all those who would follow in his footsteps will be emboldened tomorrow."

More recently, in 2002, none other than Hillary Clinton stated: "It is clear, however, that if left unchecked, Saddam Hussein will continue to increase his capacity to wage biological and chemical warfare, and will keep trying to develop nuclear weapons. Should he succeed in that endeavor, he could alter the political and security landscape of the Middle East, which as we know all too well affects American security."

Moore then moves on to the next government whopper: "Iraq has ties to Osama bin Laden and al Qaeda!" This Moore denies.

Again, Moore does his best to reduce a deeply complex issue into a few snappy sound bytes. His rebuttal consists of a reference to a February 2003 British intelligence report stating that bin Laden and Hussein had once tried to team up but found their ideologies were incompatible. Perhaps so, but war makes strange ideological bedfellows. (You don't think that Stalin, Churchill, and Roosevelt hung out at the same political clubs, do you?) Not to mention that al Qaeda doesn't have a legal monopoly on terrorism, nor does it franchise local establishments with exclusive sales territory. Richard Miniter's *Losing bin Laden* describes a terrorist summit meeting held in Iran for the purpose of promoting Iran's pet terror group, Hezbollah, as the No. 1 fellows in the field. Represented at the meeting were Hamas, Hezbollah, al Qaeda, and three branches of the Islamic Jihad. The group established a triumvirate to coordinate attacks against U.S. targets. As a compromise, the group was chaired by a Shiite, but the other two members were both Sunni.

Miniter also devotes an appendix to documented ties between al Qaeda and Hussein. Iraqi intelligence officers visited bin Laden, and bin Laden's men received training in Iraq, all of which has been well documented. Terrorists can be quite practical people. They don't necessarily pass up alliances and mutual aid because of ideological differences or personal dislikes. Al Qaeda and Hussein shared a deep hatred of the United States, George Bush, and the Saudi leadership. To put it simply: Al Qaeda hated these targets for religious reasons, Hussein for political ones, but both hated the same enemies. So why not scratch each other's backs?

And just what was Saddam doing with that camp called Salman Pak, anyway?

Chances are good that you haven't heard of Salman Pak. A bit of a news blackout there, perhaps?

Well, it seems that a couple of Iraqi officials reported after their capture that there was a camp at that location, south of Baghdad, used for training in terrorism, nicely equipped with buses and an aircraft fuselage. The facility was used both for training Iraqis and non-Iraqis (presumably visiting terrorists on sabbaticals). U.S. troops seized the place and found the buses and aircraft as described (the one discrepancy being that one Iraqi official thought the aircraft hull was from a 707, when it was actually from a Russian passenger plane).

One of the officials was Sabah Khodada, a former captain in the Iraqi army and later an intelligence officer. During an interview with PBS, Khodada declared, among other things, that "[operations at the base were] conducted by people who were trained by Saddam. And I'm going to keep assuring the world this is what happened."

In the same interview, Khodada also described in detail the training missions conducted using the hull of the plane located at the base. The training was for terrorism: "They would be trained on assassinations, kidnapping, hijacking of airplanes, hijacking of buses, public buses, hijacking of trains and all other kinds of operations related to terrorism." The aircraft fuselage was used to practice getting into the cockpit and using improvised weapons to terrorize crew and passengers. His first reaction, on hearing of 9/11, was that "this operation was conducted by people who were trained by

Saddam." The hijackers had skills that required practice, and that wasn't available in the hills of Afghanistan. It was available at Salman Pak.

The critical points here are: (1) just because Saddam and Osama didn't see eye to eye does not mean they couldn't coordinate on matters of joint interest; and (2) if Saddam didn't team up with al Qaeda, he *was* showing a very unhealthy interest in terrorism in his own right.

That brings us to Moore's famous (and capitalized, of course) proclamation:

THERE . . . IS . . . NO . . . TERRORIST . . . THREAT!

Here, Moore explains (with a welcome, if all too rare, bit of common sense) that the odds of an American being killed by a terrorist is somewhere between zero and statistically insignificant. When our time comes, what's going to get us is heart disease, cancer, other mainstream health problems.

Of course, one factor in Moore's equation that he does not acknowledge is that those sponsoring or supporting terrorism have experienced an awfully high casualty rate in recent years. What was thinkable under a President Clinton who responded to terrorism by launching a few cruise missiles into what was revealed to be an aspirin factory becomes unthinkable under a president who is liable to respond with bunker-buster bombs that can home in on a certain leader's favorite brand of Scotch.

Afghanistan, Iraq . . . who's next on the overthrow list? The terrorist-supporting nations have begun shouting: "NOT ME!"

Not Syria: "Syria has appealed to Australia to use its close ties with Washington to help the Arab nation shake off its reputation as a terrorist haven and repair its relations with the U.S."

Not Libya: "Libya has agreed to end its pursuit of weapons of mass destruction and allow international inspectors to enter the country and search for such weapons, President Bush announced Friday." It seems that Colonel Muammar Gaddafi *did* have some nuclear playthings in progress, but he's willing to fess up and hand them over. (Libya seems, if anything, to be going a bit too far in its haste to buddy up. Muammar's son, Seif al-Islam Gaddafi, has begun chastising Arab leaders: "Instead of shouting and criticizing the American initiative, you have to bring democracy to your countries, and then there will be no need to fear America or your people. . . . The Arabs should either change or change will be imposed on them from outside.")

This is being brought about by emphatic demonstrations that the United States is not only carrying a big stick but is prepared to make vigorous use of it. To Moore, of course, that is a horrifying thought. "We need to shut this insane Pandora's box Bush and Cheney have opened—the notion that it is ethical to kill people *in case* they want to attack us is not the way to relax the rest of the world. . . ." Mike can't get it through his head that when you are dealing with dangerous men, you DON'T want them to relax when they see you coming. You want them to start sweating and asking what they can do for you.

Moore goes on to point out how the FBI has used the Patriot Act to expand its powers of intrusion (and, we might add, budgets and manpower). It is a point worth making, although he fails to appreciate that the FBI's efforts to increase its power are by no means a post-9/11 phenomenon. (In fact, most of the examples he cites to illustrate FBI abuses of the Patriot Act involve neither FBI nor its Patriot Act powers. Federal agencies had considerable license to harass, annoy, and foul up before the Patriot Act became law.)

Bureaucracies are living things and will exploit causes to live and grow, regardless of the time or the administration. You can't really separate government organizations ("good") from business organizations ("bad"). Both are led by human beings, interested in power, money, promotions, and status.

If Moore really believes, as he told Robert Novak, that "[t]he Patriot Act is the first step. *Mein Kampf* was written long before Hitler came to power . . . if people don't speak up against this, you end up with something like they had in Germany" or that with another terrorist strike or two "martial law will be declared in our country and we're inching towards a police state," then he has no business touting the virtues of socialism, let alone proclaiming that "[u]ltimately, getting rid of the guns will be the answer."

Dude is, like much of Moore's work, at least good for some unintended humor.

According to Mike, Richard Nixon was the last liberal president: "Nixon was more liberal than the last five presidents we've had." In this respect, Moore probably has a bit of a point. Nixon expanded the federal bureaucracy and budget. Before him, federal criminal practice was a backwater, mostly consisting of income tax fraud cases. He created the Drug Enforcement Administration and Alcohol, Tobacco, and Firearms departments; established the Law Enforcement Assistance Administration to dole out military gear to local police; pioneered mass no-knock searches; and used the Internal Revenue Service and the Federal Bureau of Investigation to harass his opponents. Of course, the result is that today federal courts and prisons are packed to bursting (and not just with murderers, rapists, and thieves, either). What is interesting is Moore's implicit definition of *liberal:* Nixon is liberal only if liberal means any person who wants to expand the federal establishment, its powers, and its spending. Unfortunately, by that definition there is no difference between liberalism and fascism. Moore's definition essentially leaves out what many would see as the core elements of liberalism, at least pre-Clinton liberalism—things like concerns for civil liberties and protection of the individual.

Finally, in Chapter 8, Moore pledges to do something. He will contribute the limit to whichever Democratic candidate has the best chance of winning in the 2004 election. And not only the White House race. "I will give the maximum legal amount to any congressional candidate who has a chance of helping to take back the House or the Senate from the Republicans. I will write check after check until there is no more of my tax cut to spend." In fact, he proclaims, he has established a website (www.HelpSpendMikesTaxCut.com) where his fans can vote on which candidates he should donate to.

Knowing how tight Mike is with his millions, we decided to look at how well he followed through on his promise.

A January 31, 2005, check of Federal Elections Commission donation reports, for Presidential, Senate, and House races, as well as Political Action Committees, showed not a single Moore donation to any 2004 campaign. The sole Moore political donation we found was five years before to Hillary Clinton. The website (www.HelpSpendMikesTaxCut.com) is, by the way, closed up.

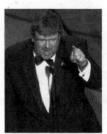

AND THE OSCAR FOR ACTING OUT GOES TO . . .

*A*uthors' note: This is not one of those books where an author attempts a psychiatric analysis based on inadequate training and limited experience with the person being studied. The authors in this case have no psychoanalytical training whatsoever and have never met the person under study.

With that disclaimer attached, one textbook disorder did pop into mind during our study of Michael Moore.

NARCISSISM

At risk of oversimplification: Freud, who defined the Narcissistic Personality Disorder, concluded that development of a normal human follows a certain path. In the womb, the infant is unconscious of any world beyond himself. Birth changes this: The baby suddenly feels hunger, cold, and diaper chafe.

At first, the infant still sees himself as the entire universe. His parents are viewed simply as extensions of himself, existing only to fulfill his needs and desires. Since the baby *is* the universe, his perceptions are the only reality. And of course, all gratifications of his desires must be immediate.

In terms of personality development, the narcissist stops right here. He (it is predominantly a male trait) remains the universe, surrounded by others who exist only as tools to fulfill his desires.

Objective measures of truth and the external world never register to a narcissist. Thus, meaning (of an event, a comment, anything) is determined solely by how it makes the narcissist *feel*. So while the adult narcissist has learned the shell of adult language, representations, and behavior, his interactions with others are severely stunted—he can only view people as tools that serve or oppose his wishes.

The American Psychiatric Association defines the disorder in these words: A pervasive pattern of grandiosity (in fantasy or behavior), need for admiration, and lack of empathy, beginning by early adulthood and present in a variety of contexts, as indicated by five (or more) of the following:

1. *Has a grandiose sense of self-importance*

That's our boy! The only fellow (apart from prophets and evangelists) who has written a chapter in the almighty voice of God (Chapter 6 of *Dude, Where's My Country?* begins: "Hi. God here.").

As Dr. Sam Vaknin notes in his book *Malignant Self Love: Narcissism Revisited*, "The narcissist never talks—he lectures." Moore was even unable to receive an Academy Award without delivering a lecture! Typically, on receipt of such a prestigious award, the honoree welcomes the opportunity to thank those who made his work possible. But gratitude runs directly counter to the narcissist's feelings of entitlement: The contributions of others are only what Moore deserves. Why share the glory by rewarding that which deserves no reward?

2. *Is preoccupied with fantasies of unlimited success, power* . . .

That's Mike, again. In the 2000 elections, he backed Nader and then bragged to the world that Gore's campaign was begging him to abandon Nader and save them from disaster. In Moore's open letter to Gore, he chastises the former vice president: "Look, Al, you have screwed up—big time. . . . And now your people are calling ME, asking ME to do the job YOU'VE failed to do! Jeez, I've got enough on my plate these days, between work and the holidays coming up and the leaves I should be raking—and now I'm supposed to save YOU? Unbelievable!"

It's unbelievable, all right.

Never mind that Moore didn't seem particularly important to anyone during the presidential election cycle of 2000. As he recounts in *Stupid White Men*, when Moore tried to reach Nader on the telephone, he wound up talking to staffers; the most he could hope for was that the candidate was silently listening in: "I . . . was aware there was a chance the man himself was listening in." *Note to Mike:* If anyone *really* thinks you can carry a key state for them, they don't let staffers field your call; and if they are on the line, they aren't silent. Candidates, of all people, know what to kiss and when. If a fellow can deliver Michigan to them—or for that matter Idaho or Delaware—they grab the phone and pucker up.

And of course there is Moore's other grandiose plan. He joined the NRA so that he could have his supporters elect him as president of the organization—a campaign that would merely require 5 million or so Moorites to become life members, at a cost of $750 each, and then cast a vote for him. (First things first: Moore should have checked out the process by which the NRA's president is elected—The vote is cast by the board of directors, not the organization's members.)

3. *Believes that he or she is "special" and unique and can only be understood by (or associate with) other "special" or unique or high-status people (or institutions)*

It is doubtful that anyone in the history of the human race has written as many "Open Letters" to major figures from George W. Bush and Al Gore, to Yasser Arafat. Where other authors might use an open letter to appeal to the recipient's better nature and encourage change, Moore's letters almost invariably berate and heckle his recipients, treating them as his inferiors.

An amusing insight: Dr. Vaknin points out that the narcissist often expects and feels entitled "to talk directly to authority figures (and not their assistants or secretaries)." And the plot of *Roger & Me* was . . .

4. *Requires excessive admiration*

For all his ego and mendacity, Moore is *immensely* popular. He's got an Oscar, more film awards than we can easily count, and a following whose blindest followers resemble cult members. Like a cult, the Moore movement shares the drive to recruit converts (we are informed that at least one university has made Bowling required viewing for all Freshman English students, and elsewhere many teachers have done the same on their own). The Moore Phenomenon is certainly widespread. And as we've seen over and over again, almost everyone who dares not to "excessively admire" Moore is attacked personally and viciously. Harlan Jacobson, one example from a long list, faced such a backlash from Moore after exposing the inaccuracies of *Roger & Me* that he withdrew from film criticism for a time.

5. *Has a sense of entitlement, that is, unreasonable expectations of especially favorable treatment or automatic and full compliance with his or her expectations*

Douglas Urbanski, his former Hollywood manager, told the *Times* of London how Moore was the only client he fired in writing. "Michael Moore would never withstand the scrutiny he lays on other people," Urbanksi said.

One of Moore's employees at *TV Nation* was more blunt. "For the preservation of my own soul I have to consider him as just an entertainer," he explained, "because otherwise he's a huge asshole. If you consider him an entertainer, then his acting like a selfish, self-absorbed, pouty, deeply conflicted, easily wounded child is run-of-the-mill, standard behavior. But if he's a political force, then he's a jerk and a hypocrite. . . ."

Another example, drawn from the *New York Post:* during a speaking engagement at London's Roundhouse Theater, a petulant Moore launched into a tirade against the staff. He "stormed around all day screaming at everyone, even the 5 pound-an-hour bar staff, telling them how we were all con men and useless. Then he went on stage and did it in public." Moore apologized only after the staff essentially boycotted him, refusing even to open the doors to the public.

6. *Is "interpersonally exploitative," that is, uses others to achieve his or her own ends*

This is Moore, again, no doubt about it. Daniel Radosh summed it up in his 1997 *Salon* article: "Michael Moore is phenomenally good at one thing: getting people to make idiots of themselves on camera."

Moore's movies are littered with people he talks into an interview and then exploits, portraying them as crass or ignorant and using them to highlight his own superiority. The manner in which he wheedles Heston in *Bowling for Columbine*—pretending to be an NRA member wanting to drop by for a friendly talk and filming—is a classic example. Another is the way he suckered his then-friend Larry Stecco into appearing in *Roger & Me*, then edited the footage to make Stecco, an attorney devoted to helping the poor, look like a spokesman for the brainless and wealthy.

7. *Lacks empathy, is unwilling to recognize or identify with the feelings and needs of others*

This is not just a personal lack of empathy. The narcissist *simply cannot understand* when he has fouled up or put his foot in his mouth socially because he cannot understand that other people may see things differently. His feelings are the universe and the only reality.

Moore has a long and sordid history of posting screeds that make anyone with the smallest capacity for empathy immediately cringe. The narcissist would rather be notorious than be ignored. Take, as an example, his "Open Letter to Elian Gonzalez," a tirade that appeared on his web site during 2000. In this case, he berates not Elian, but the mother who died trying to escape Cuba with him. She kidnapped him and placed his life in "horrible jeopardy," Moore writes to Gonzalez, adding, "The truth is your mother and her boyfriend snatched you and put you on that death boat because they simply wanted to make more money."

At times Moore's insensitivity has even alienated those who would otherwise be considered supporters. In an interview with FoxNews.com columnist Roger Friedman, "South Park" co-creator Matt Stone lamented Moore's cruel mistreatment of Charlton Heston in *Bowling for Columbine:* "It's hard to make Heston look sympathetic, but Moore did it. You can't help but think this is an 80-year-old man with Alzheimer's. He looked so frail."

Moore responded in a different way to word of Heston's ailment: "[Heston] doesn't have Alzheimer's. He says he has Alzheimer's-like symptoms." The *New York Post* quoted Moore's response and summed it up nicely: "Moore doesn't quit while he's behind."

Precisely! This event and Moore's reaction to it are especially significant. We all frequently act out of self-interest; we all occasionally behave egocentrically or narcissistically. The difference is that most of us can perceive when we're behaving this way and retreat from dysfunction before it starts to define our personalities.

Moore's inability to recognize his own most egregious narcissistic lapses is very significant. Yes, Moore can't quit when he's behind—not out of stubbornness, but because he doesn't see that he's screwed up royally. His view is the only view, and people simply *must* see that—or they fall into the "nation of idiots."

8. *Is often envious of others or believes that others are envious of him or her*

In Moore's view, the world doesn't operate by cooperation, friendship, or loyalty. It is comprised of rats clawing their way to the top; and to succeed, one must tear down the other rats.

If someone gets hurt in the process—Larry Stecco, Charlton Heston, whoever—tough. They would have done the same. (Could it be coincidence that Moore named his film production firm "Dog Eat Dog Productions?")

Moore finds others envying him wherever he goes. In Flint, pure spite stopped the conservative town newspaper from praising his success. He complained to the Onion AV Club that "[t]he local paper in Flint has never written the words, 'and he lives in a beautiful apartment on the Upper West Side of Manhattan,' because the local paper in Flint hates me."

Yet in the same interview, Moore also explained how his new, liberal neighbors in New York are also jealous of his success. "They never mention [the New York home] in Flint. But I'll read it in the liberal publications. . . . They're just pissed because they're not sitting in this apartment." The writers of these articles, he adds, are "grunts" at *Newsweek* or the *New Yorker,* and probably live in "a five floor walk-up down in the East Village." So, continues Moore, "There's a voice in their head, the voice of class, screaming, [adopts whining voice] 'Not fair! Not fair!'"

Dr. Sam Vaknin outlines the essential envy component of narcissism: "The suppression of envy is at the CORE of the narcissist's being. . . . If there are others out there who are better than he—he envies them, he lashes out at them ferociously, uncontrollably, madly, hatefully and spitefully."

Moore's long list of imagined rivals—the others he is constantly raging against—include former Vice President Al Gore, President George Bush, former NRA president Charlton Heston . . . not to mention the twelve pages he spends in *Stupid White Men* just running down (in both senses of the term) the current administration's Cabinet.

9. *Shows arrogant, haughty behaviors or attitudes*

Celebrities, once they reach a certain strata of fame, are often capable of making income just by being celebrities. Moore is a classic example, as he's now giving lectures to col leges across the country for tens of thousands a pop.

Matt Hirsch, a Cornell student, saw this aspect of Moore when he protested Moore's fee (then only $10,000) by presenting him with an oversized check in that amount, and pointed out that he'd charged more for a few hours of time than some teaching assistants were paid in a year.

It was, if anything, a classic Moore stunt. But Moore exploded. "Motherfucker. . . . You come down with your check making a big-ass statement," he shouted, according to the Cornell *Daily Sun*, "I give this money away to organizations I support . . ."

Moore's rabid anger, and his attempt to humiliate the student, illustrates yet another related aspect of narcissism. "The narcissist is seething with enmity and venom," Dr. Vaknin points out. The venom can appear explosively when the narcissist is challenged. When Moore's veracity was criticized by Joe Scarborough, a commentator and Florida congressman, Moore dug for dirt until he discovered that one of Scarborough's female aides had been found dead in his Congressional office (the coroner's ruling was heart attack). Moore then began telling his audiences that he had reserved the internet domain name www.joescarboroughkilledhisintern.com, leaving them to guess what would be posted to it. (In fact, the site remains empty to this day—though it is owned by Moore's production company). He later told the New Yorker that his accusation of murder was "just kidding around." This did not stop him from hinting that Scarborough was a

MICHAEL MOORE IS A BIG FAT STUPID WHITE MAN

murderer, telling the reporter that the coroner was incompetent and asking her "Wasn't it strange that a twenty-eight-year-old girl who went running regularly should drop dead of a heart condition?" Apparently to Moore no conduct is too vile when it is directed at one who dares to question his stance.

In another college appearance, this time at Humboldt State University in California, Moore was asked by a reporter about small businesses being taken over by chain stores.

Moore replied with a bombastic, deeply personal rant against small business, replying that in Flint small businesses "supported all the right-wing groups." Moore, the anticorporate activist, was on a roll. "The small hardware salesman, the small clothing store salespersons, Jesse the Barber who signed his name three different times on three different petitions to recall me from the school board. Fuck all these small businesses—fuck 'em all! Bring in the chains. The small businesspeople are the rednecks that run the town and suppress [sic] the people. Fuck 'em all."

This display indicates a truly pathological degree of self-absorption. A fall-out with "Jesse the Barber," who dared defy Moore in a piddling squabble thirty years before, constitutes sufficient grounds to determine all issues relating to small businesses vs. chain stores.

One of the aspects of this haughtiness is the narcissist's feeling that he is above the law (the law is for *der untermensch!*), Moore's got that angle covered as well. As the *New York Times* has reported, although Moore was famous for bothering others, he apparently didn't care for being bothered himself. After Moore fired Alan Edelstein, Edelstein took a play from Moore's playbook and began following Moore with a videocamera, trying to corner him into an interview. "Mr. Moore responded by filing a complaint with the New York police accusing Mr. Edelstein of aggravated harassment, menacing and criminal trespassing," the *Times* article reported, and "As a result, Mr. Edelstein was arrested in March and spent nine hours in a cell at the Midtown North police station."

A narcissistic personality can have an even darker side, which Dr. Vaknin describes as a "burning desire, nay need, to be punished. In the grotesque mind of the narcissist, his punishment is equally his vindication. By being permanently on trial, the narcissist claims the high moral ground and the position of the martyr. . . ."

And Moore fits that bill. There's no question that he views his attacks on others (no matter how nasty or scurrilous) as a crusade, while others' criticism of him are character assassination and persecution.

Let's look again at a particularly conspicuous example: Moore's account of the police raid at his book-signing event for *Stupid White Men.* As Moore wrote, "I'm in San Diego, and I have just escaped being arrested by the San Diego police." He was signing books when he heard a commotion and saw people scattering. "The San Diego police are coming down the aisle, their large flashlights out [the auditorium lights are still on, so we all understand the implied 'other' use of these instruments]." The officers begin shouting threats: "'VACATE THESE PREMISES IMMEDIATELY OR YOU WILL ALL BE ARRESTED!' I cannot believe what I am hearing. 'YOU WILL NOT RECEIVE ANOTHER WARNING. LEAVE NOW—OR FACE ARREST!'"

Moore attempts to reason with the brutish officers and is told "I don't care what you are doing—this is your last warning. I am ready to arrest you and everyone else."

Phew . . . in just a few paragraphs, Moore manages to expose a deep network of corruption and oppression brewing in the San Diego police department. Or is it that a larger force is at work—those nefarious henchmen of George W. Bush?

Unfortunately for Moore, one of the fans present at the event writes his own account, stating that he was astonished to read Moore's own description of the episode.

Kynn Bartlett gives a very different explanation of what happened. Sponsors of the book signing rented the auditorium until 11 P.M. As the magic hour approached, the janitors pointed out that they had to stay late and clean things up, so punctuality would be appreciated. Imposing on the working-class janitors was apparently of no concern to Moore, who according to Bartlett's account, kept on signing books after 11 P.M. came and went. After a while the janitors got fed up with waiting and called the police, two of whom showed up.

Bartlett describes the affair after the police arrived. Two officers came in, "and rather decent ones at that, doing an uncomfortable task." They announced the use permit for the event had expired, and everyone had to leave. "The cops didn't come off as abusive, but rather as matter-of-fact and straightforward," writes Kynn, "They didn't act like they were there to arrest droves of people for trespassing."

The narcissist alert is flashing throughout the San Diego episode. First, Moore has no concern for the janitors who understandably want to get home before midnight. Second, he has no idea that this imposition on them might have consequences—they're just supposed to sit there and take it. Third, Moore takes any opportunity—or in this case, fakes any opportunity—to play the martyr. Two polite cops telling him his time is up and he has to leave become in Moore's mind a pair of thugs, out to threaten and imprison (or even beat) him and his followers. And the discrepancy between the two accounts shows how easily Moore will take a episode that seemed innocent to one of his fans and spin it to play the persecuted martyr.

In our humble and nonprofessional opinions, Moore certainly resembles the walking textbook definition for Narcissistic Personality Disorder—and his millions of adoring fans ("Mike's Militia," as some have titled themselves) aren't helping the case.

Ok, Mike, up off the couch. This session's on the house.

FAHRENHEIT 9/11: THE TEMPERATURE AT WHICH TRUTH GOES TO HELL IN A HANDBASKET

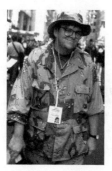

In 2004, Michael Moore unveiled his crowning work. At the very least, it crowned his narcissism-infected dream world.

The Oscar for best documentary, or the Cannes *Palme d'Or*, were unworthy objectives for his stature. Instead, Moore proclaimed, the target of *Fahrenheit 9/11* would be to change the course of the upcoming presidential election and topple the administration of his enemy George W. Bush. Immediately after that triumph, he would march onward to secure the Oscar, not merely for Best Documentary, but for Best Picture of the Year.

Things didn't quite go according to plan. Mistakes were made, to use the words of Richard Nixon. One heartland Republican leader noted that every time Moore endorsed Kerry, Kerry's numbers plummeted. Leon Panetta, chief of staff to former President Bill Clinton, noted in dismay that, "The party of FDR has become the party of Michael Moore and that doesn't help the party."

As Moore pursued the Democratic cause, the Democrats fled in the other direction. It was probably the first time that Moore won a footrace. Moore's claim that Senator Daschle attended a screening and gratefully hugged Moore got greater play than Daschle's response that he'd done no such thing.

On January 21, 2005, George W. Bush was inaugurated for his second term. Senator Daschle became former Senator Daschle. Four days later, the Academy denied *Fahrenheit 9/11* so much as an Oscar nomination.

Perhaps it was Hollywood payback for having failed in his electoral objectives. Or perhaps the Academy simply lacked the right category: Best Propaganda Film.

"Propaganda" is in most cases just an easily-hurled pejorative. In the case of *Fahrenheit 9/11*, however, the term may be applied with scientific precision; it has all of the attributes, uses all of the tools that modern theories of propaganda demand. Before we undertake a detailed refutation of *Fahrenheit*'s theses, let's take a look at those tools.

1. DECEPTION, BUT NEVER QUITE LIES

The modern theory of propaganda holds that the spokesman should never actually speak a black-and-white lie, but should strive to create a false conclusion nonetheless. The spokesman, thus, can never quite be "caught in a lie." He can always evade with claims that he didn't mean to create that impression.

Bowling for Columbine showed that Moore is a master at this, and *Fahrenheit* confirms the impression. When Moore is forced into a corner, his first defense is that he didn't really say that, or didn't mean to create that idea. In *Fahrenheit*, Moore proclaims that the United States attacked Sadaam's regime despite the fact that it had never threatened the United States nor murdered an American citizen. When ABC's Jake Tapper pointed out that the regime quite clearly had killed Americans, had given shelter to Abu Nidal and other terrorists who had killed Americans, and had tried to assassinate former President Bush with a bomb, Moore replied, "That isn't what I said," pointed out that he had said "murdered" rather than killed and that "nothing you just said is proof that the Iraqi government ever murdered an American citizen."

The distinction between "murdered" and "killed," "attempted to murder," and "was an accessory to murder" is perhaps a technical one, when the question is whether Sadaam's regime was attacked without provocation, but it enables Moore as narrator to evade, however technically, the charge of lying. His words, narrowly and precisely construed, were perhaps not entirely false. If the listener got the wrong impression that an attack on Iraq was unprovoked, that is the listener's problem, not Moore's.

Further, since the question is the viewer's impressions, if caught the propagandist can simply disavow any *intent* to mislead. After all, if misleading was not his intent, then the error is properly charged to the viewer's mistake. Since intent is a mental state, no one save a telepath can disprove the propagandist's claim.

An example that we will explore in greater depth below: in *Fahrenheit* Moore works hard to create the impression that in the days immediately after September 11, 2001, when civilian flying was forbidden, President Bush permitted members of the bin Laden family who were living in the United States to fly out of the country. While footage of singer Ricky Martin, trapped in a chaos-filled airport is shown, Moore narrates: "Not even Ricky Martin would fly. But really, who wanted to fly? No one. Except the bin Ladens." Cut to footage of a departing aircraft zooming past, as Moore talks about the White House permitting Saudis, including bin Laden relatives, to fly out of the country in the days after 9/11, and a former FBI agent says the Bureau should have been allowed to interview them before they departed.

The 9/11 Commission Staff Report and Richard Clarke (whom Moore's film depicted as a hero) refuted these claims—no one had flown during the no-fly ban, the bin Laden family members didn't leave until nearly two weeks after 9/11, the FBI questioned everyone it wanted to, and Clarke, not Bush, authorized their departure.

When the *Washington Post* called for Moore's reaction to this news, Moore had the modern propagandist's escape— while he had in fact created the false impression, and spent considerable effort to do so, he could still claim that was not his intent. The *Post* printed Moore's lame defense: "Joanne Doroshow, an associate producer of *Fahrenheit 9/11*, said Moore did not intend to suggest that the bin Ladens flew away while civilian flights were grounded."

2. DOCTORING OF FOOTAGE TO REMOVE CONTEXT, THEN SEQUENCING IT WITH OTHER INFORMATION SO AS TO CREATE A NEW, DECEPTIVE, CONTEXT

We might call this decontextualization and recontextualization. It goes beyond merely taking something out of context. Instead, once the true context has been removed, it is replaced by a new and invented context. *Bowling for Columbine* showcased Moore's grasp of this propaganda technique as he took Charlton Heston's pre-election speech and convinced viewers that it was a speech given in reaction to events that had occurred months before. *Fahrenheit* shows that Moore has moved beyond a grasp of the propagandist's tool to a mastery of it. A few examples follow.

Moore obtained footage of a February 28, 2003 press conference with Secretary of Defense Donald Rumsfeld. One topic is negotiation of an anti-terrorism program involving the United States and Philippines; Rumsfeld explains that we "are still in the process of discussing exactly how we ought to do that and what shape it ought to take . . ." A reporter tells Rumsfeld that he had been told last week that the program had been agreed upon. Rumsfeld responds that he had made no such statement and suggests that the media ought to be more careful about verifying rumors before running them.

Q: But again, we were told that that was agreed upon.

RUMSFELD: You weren't told by me.

Q: Well—

RUMSFELD: I mean, you're going to be told lots of things. You get told things every day that don't happen. It doesn't seem to bother people. They don't—it's printed in the press. The world thinks all these things happen. They never happened. It's—everyone's so eager to get the story before, in fact, the story's there that the world is constantly being fed things that haven't happened. All I can tell you is, it hasn't happened, it's going to happen, and we're worrying through those issues in a very constructive, friendly, positive way.

From this exchange, Moore takes the footage of "You get told things every day that don't happen. It doesn't seem to bother people." He then places it in a section of the movie devoted to claims that the Bush Administration is misleading the public about the war in Iraq. In its real context, Rumsfeld is complaining that the media is running incorrect stories based on rumor. In the context that Moore has created, Rumsfeld seems to be telling reporters that they will get lied to every day and had best get used to it.

Another example of decontextualization and recontextualization: Moore secures footage of 9/11 Commission chairman Thomas Kean. Filmed in July 2003, Kean is complaining that while the White House is cooperative with the Commission, some agencies are not:

> [W]e've—if you look at the report that we issued yesterday, we go down agency by agency by agency, all through the administration. And in some of those agencies, the cooperation is quite good, and we got a number of things that we needed. In other agencies, where in some cases we've made massive requests, we haven't gotten the materials we needed, and we certainly haven't gotten them in a timely fashion; the deadlines we've set have passed. We've got our own deadline; by statue, we've got to report by next May. So we can't brook that kind of thing. We've got to get the information we need to do our work. So while I think the White House is cooperating, I think they're trying to do their best to help us in a number of ways, some agencies, led at the moment by the Department of Defense, are not cooperating to the extent we need that cooperation. Now, it's better than it was, and it's moving in the right direction. But the next two or three weeks are going to be vital. Talk to me in another two or three weeks.

Moore also secured footage of President Bush telling Tim Russert of MSNBC on February 13, 2004 that:

> We have given extraordinary cooperation with Chairmen Kean and Hamilton. As you know, we made an agreement on what's called, "Presidential Daily Briefs," so they could see the information the CIA provided me . . .

The two statements are, of course, consistent (quite apart from the fact that Bush's statement that the administration has been cooperative comes nearly a year after Kean's statement that "things are moving in the right direction").

But Moore creates a new context. First, he informs the viewer (correctly) that President Bush had opposed the creation of the 9/11 Commission. Then he notes (correctly again—the modern propagandist knows he must never *speak* a lie) that twenty-eight pages were redacted from the report. Then he cuts to the *2004* Bush interview, sliced to one sentence of Bush saying, "We have given extraordinary cooperation with Chairmen Kean and Hamilton," followed by two sentences from Kean's *2003* footage: "We haven't gotten the materials we needed, and we certainly haven't gotten them in a timely fashion. The deadlines we set have passed."

By stripping the context—Kean's statement had said the White House was cooperating, but Defense was not—and switching the order (Kean would ultimately say that "we had wonderful access in the end. I mean, we were able to see every single document we requested . . .") Moore makes President Bush seem a liar. Moore creates a completely false impression—all without uttering a false word himself.

Another example of how Moore employs the changing of context relates to the government of Afghanistan, installed by the United States after it overthrew the Taliban. The interim president was Hamid Karzai. Karzai was the son of the head of a Pushtun tribe, had been a leader in the Afghan fight against the Soviet occupation, had been Deputy Foreign Minister before breaking with the Taliban over its support of terror. Some considered him the most visible Pushtun leader against the Taliban, and after its fall he chaired an interim government of Afghan tribes.

The United States then appointed as its ambassador to the new government one Zalmay Khalizad, an Afghan who held a Ph.D. from the University of Chicago, and had taught political science at Columbia. He had created the RAND Center for Middle Eastern Studies, and served as Assistant Deputy Undersecretary of Defense and as advisor to the president.

In context, both appointments seem rational, even exceptionally wise. So Moore strips away the context and inserts a different one: "Who was Hamid Karzai? He was a former advisor to Unocal. Bush also appointed as his envoy to Afghanistan Zalmay Khalilzad who was also a former Unocal advisor." David Kopel, in the following chapter, demonstrates that these men were not in fact former Unocal advisors. But the critical point here is that by removing the context of the appointments, and inserting another invented context, Moore creates the impression that the two were appointed to please an oil company, if not to ensure Afghanistan would be a puppet to American oil profiteering.

Elsewhere in *Fahrenheit,* Moore is content to strip an event from context, and use it to frame a question that the viewer's mind must answer. While the answer would have been clear if the context were retained, the isolation of the event lets Moore direct the reader's mind toward assuming an incorrect (and often somewhat paranoid) conclusion. One example is the Bush administration's attempts before September 11 to use diplomacy to deal with bin Laden (an approach which the pacifist Moore would surely approve). The administration had informed the Taliban that it would be held accountable for any bin Laden attacks, pressed them to turn bin Laden over for justice, and renewed covert aid to the Taliban's opponent, the Northern Alliance. As part of that effort, when Taliban representative Sayed Hashemi visited the United States in March 2001, "The administration rejected his claim that the Taliban had complied with U.S. requests to isolate Osama bin Laden and affirmed its nonrecognition of the Taliban."

Moore simply removes all context. He notes that the envoy visited the United States, and says that the Bush administration "welcomed" him "to tour the United States to help improve the image of the Taliban." He then asks the viewer, "Why on Earth did the Bush administration allow a Taliban leader to visit the United States, knowing that the Taliban were harboring the man who bombed the U.S. Cole and our African embassies?"

Coming as it does, right after a segment in which Moore creates the false impression that President Bush was trying to convince the Taliban to allow a natural gas pipeline which (again, falsely) is seen as benefiting Enron, the impression created is that the Administration was still "buttering up" the Taliban to benefit Bush's financial supporters: it would even consort with killers of Americans, if it stood to gain blood money for Enron! The impression is completely false—and Moore creates it without uttering a false word (except perhaps "welcomed," which is at least ambiguous). Again, if cornered,

Moore can employ the "I never really said that, you jumped to the conclusion on your own" defense.

3. MANIPULATION OF SEQUENCE

Moore is, as *Roger & Me* and *Bowling for Columbine* showed, a master at this tool of propaganda. Entirely ordinary footage can be cut and spliced to change the order of events, or to make the propagandist's target look stupid, callous, or bumbling. Making the target look callous can be as simple as taking a tragic, heartrending scene and adding footage of the target laughing or enjoying himself (the required footage can come from before the tragedy, or years after: the audience is not told, and the emotional impact is the same).

Moore employed the "make the target look callous" approach on Charlton Heston in *Bowling,* and he does the same in *Fahrenheit*—the Lipscombs speak movingly of losing their son, asking, "And for what?" whereupon Moore cuts to a cheerful, upbeat, Halliburton commercial, or footage of an Iraqi child receiving surgery fades into a government official speaking of how precisely targeted the bombing is. But in *Fahrenheit* he branches into new applications of the tactic. His central theme is that President Bush is a goof-off, so footage of Bush golfing is put to use. He splices together an interviewee saying that it took two months to clear the part of Afghanistan where bin Laden was believed to be hiding, then Moore asks, "A mass murderer who attacked the United States was given a two-month head start? Who in their right mind would do that?" and then cuts to footage of Bush hitting a drive and asking, "Anybody say 'nice shot?'"

Probably the most impressive use of this technique, though, comes when Moore argues that the administration is manipulating the public through issuing confusing messages on the danger of terror, switching the terror alert levels up and down. Moore has the following footage at his disposal.

President Bush in 2001, giving a stump speech for a Congressional candidate: "It's important to have a senator and a President and people in Washington, D.C., who see the world really the way it is, not the way we wish it would be. And the world is changed after September the 11th. It's changed because we're no longer safe from potential threats overseas. It used to be that oceans could protect us. It used to be that we could sit back and say, well, we're a protected continent because of two vast oceans. We learned a tough lesson on September the 11th."

President Bush in 2001, explaining to airline workers that the Administration was increasing airport security, radically increasing the number of federal air marshals on flights, and seeing to the reinforcement of cockpit doors. He says of the terrorists that, "When they struck, they wanted to create an atmosphere of fear. And one of the great goals of this nation's war is to restore public confidence in the airline industry, is to tell the traveling public: 'Get on board. Do your business around the country. Fly and enjoy America's great destination spots. Go down to Disney World in Florida, take your families and enjoy life the way we want it to be enjoyed.'"

Secretary of Defense Rumsfeld in 2003, explaining to a meeting of former members of Congress why we cannot always wait to act on intelligence until the proof is 100% clear: "In our new security environment, the consequences of failing to act until all the dots are connected might not be 3,000 lives, but 30,000 or 300,000. We've entered into what could very well prove to be the most dangerous security environment the world has known. In the 20th century, when we, the formers, served in the Congress, we were dealing, for the most part, with a situation where, if we miscalculated, we could take the attack, take a deep breath, mobilize our forces, and go out and defeat the attackers."

Vice President Cheney in 2003, speaking to the Heritage Foundation, regarding information uncovered in Afghanistan: "And we know to a certainty that terrorists are doing everything they can to gain even deadlier means of striking us. From the training manuals we found in the caves of Afghanistan to the interrogations of terrorists that we've captured, we have learned of their ambitions to develop or acquire chemical, biological, or nuclear weapons."

The speeches are on different subjects, and span two years, but Moore chops short segments from each and mixes them to create the impression that the terror alert level is indeed being juggled to manipulate the public. First, he puts on Rep. Jim McDermott to complain that, "Well, you make them afraid by creating an aura of endless threat. They played us like an organ." He adds, "They raised the orange up to red and then they dropped it back to orange." Then Moore cuts to his sliced and diced footage from the above speeches:

PRESIDENT BUSH: The world has changed after September the 11th. It's changed because we're no longer safe. / Fly and enjoy America's great destination spots.

SECRETARY RUMSFELD: We've entered into what may very well prove to be the most dangerous security environment the world has known.

PRESIDENT BUSH: Take your families and enjoy life.

VP CHENEY: Terrorists are doing everything they can to gain even deadlier means of striking us.

PRESIDENT BUSH: Get down to Disney World in Florida.

Moore's radical splicing of the four speeches shows his mastery of timing, also. The information is hurled at you; the entire sequence takes barely over twenty seconds. There is no time to think; thinking is not what a propagandist wants of you. There is only time to form an impression: Moore is right, the administration is using the threat of terror to bewilder and manipulate us.

4. THE IN-GROUP/OUT-GROUP MANIPULATION

Others have noted how *Fahrenheit* employs the Saudis in specific, and Arabs in general, as its "bad guys"—outsiders, foreigners, perhaps even conspirators, and then repeatedly associates the Bush administration with them. Some have even gone so far as to accuse Moore of racism in this regard (although a truer comparison would be to the nativist and know-nothing movements of the nineteenth century).

In a brilliant analysis of Moore's technique, Dr. Kelton Rhoads (a social psychologist and creator of www.working-psychology.com, who is authoring a book on propaganda) points out that this is a standard propaganda technique. The propagandist creates an out-group, a "them." (The Nazis obviously did this with Jews and Slavs, but studies have shown you can create entirely artificial out-groups, and convince the in-group that they are superior to or must be suspicious of, the out-group and all who associate with them.)

In Moore's case, guys in Arab robes become the out-group, the suspicious strangers who are probably "up to something." The repeated footage of Bush associating with them, laughing with them, even holding hands with them (a common gesture of friendship between Arab males, but one that appears strange to American eyes) is employed to ensure that the viewer unconsciously associates Bush with the suspicious outsiders. Moore caps the impression with his question, "Is it rude to suggest that when the Bush family wakes up in the morning they might be thinking about what's best for the Saudis instead of what's best for you?"

5. DAMNED IF YOU DO, DAMNED IF YOU DON'T

We have noted in previous chapters that Moore's positions are often contradictory. He has elsewhere argued that the United States had no business invading Afghanistan, which would lead to the deaths of innocents, but in *Fahrenheit* he claims that Bush erred by not sending in more men and fighting more forcefully. In the movie, he criticizes the administration for having drummed up irrational fears of terrorists, and also for not doing enough to protect the Oregon coast against the risk of their amphibious onslaught. In *Dude, Where's My Country?* he claims that Osama bin Laden couldn't have been the mastermind of the September 11 attacks—he's in a cave on a dialysis machine—and in *Fahrenheit* he criticizes the Bush administration for not capturing him.

Dr. Kelton points out that another difference between a principled critic and a propagandist is that the latter will ruthlessly employ what he terms the EWYGS trap—Either Way You Go You're Screwed. No matter what the propagandist's target did, the propagandist chooses another option and claims it would have been the only good approach. Attack the Taliban, don't attack the Taliban—whatever choice Bush makes, pick the other and claim the former was a mark of stupidity or incompetence. If diplomacy is not exhausted, cite that as a mark of reckless use of violence. If diplomacy is used, state that your target "welcomed" the enemy envoyo.

In short, Moore has mastered all the tools of the twenty-first century propagandist. All Moore lacked for an Oscar run with *Fahrenheit 9/11* was a new film category: Propaganda. In that class of movie, his new creation would have won hands-down. He employs every tool and technique of the propagandist and in a truly brilliant manner.

The only problem is that he's working for the wrong side. Let us move from technique to content, and take a look at a few of the more glaring errors of his creation.

ELECTION 2000: GORE REALLY WON

Fahrenheit begins with (one more) re-run of the disputed election of 2000. In Moore's revision of history, Gore actually would have won the recount. The story is taken almost verbatim from Moore's book *Dude, Where's My Country?* to the point where we might wonder whether Moore paid himself for the film rights. In our chapter on *Dude,* and in the following chapter by David Kopel, Moore's electoral fantasies are put to rest. But it should be noted that this section of the film contains a truly remarkable act of deception.

To reinforce the viewer's impression that Gore would have won if the recounts had proceeded, Moore flashes upon the screen a headline reading: "LATEST FLORIDA RECOUNT SHOWS BUSH WON ELECTION."

Stuart K. Hayashi, a writer and blogger, found the headline interesting and decided to investigate further. Freeze-framing the image, he found the masthead of the newspaper was *The Pantagraph*, of Bloomington Illinois, and the date was December 5, 2001.

Inquiry through a librarian—who happened to be a Moore supporter at that point—determined that there was no such headline in the newspaper on that date. Casting around to other nearby dates resolved the mystery. There had been a letter to the editor, published with that as a title, on December 10, 2001. A *letter to the editor*, not a news report, let alone a headline. In fact, the author of the letter was protesting what *was* the *Pantagraph*'s position—an article stating that a consortium of news outlets had undertaken a study of the election and concluded that Bush had won. He in particular objected to the *Pantagraph*'s conclusion that, "the analysis doesn't just validate the outcome of the 2000 election, it validates the American system."

What did Moore have to do to create his supposed headline story? It took more than an edit of the image. The letter to the editor, and its title, are but one column wide. If Moore simply took the image and stretched it out, the letters would be hopelessly distorted, elongated by 300%. Instead, he had to typeset the letter to the editor anew, converting the title to headline size, and creating below it three blurred rows of supposedly supporting but unreadable text. You can't even trust Moore to show you a newspaper headline!

GEORGE W. BUSH IS SECRETLY TIED TO THE BIN LADEN FAMILY

One of the central theses of *Fahrenheit 9/11* is that President George W. Bush is awash in secret, nefarious ties to the bin

Laden family and, thereby, Osama bin Laden himself. This is no doubt a powerful, dramatic theme to organize a documentary around. After all, is there a more vicious or attention-grabbing way to bring down a president than to devote two hours of film to tying him to the most infamous mass murderer of recent history, while terrorizing your audience with fears about a secret New World Order?

But Moore's thesis has problems—big problems. First off, the bin Laden family is enormous in size, most of them are pro-Western and have useful power in a part of the world where we are short of allies. Second, it's quite important to note that the bin Laden family has long since disowned Osama. (Not too surprising: he's declared that Arab moderates and particularly Saudis are heretics and traitors to Islam. He takes particular offense at the proliferation of U.S. bases in Saudi Arabia—and bin Laden construction firms are building many of them. Denouncing one's family as worthy of death doesn't do wonders for family ties.) Knowing these facts, Moore sought guilt by association instead, implying that the entire bin Laden family is tainted by Osama's actions.

Sometimes Moore's conspiracy web stretches to the snapping point, such as his claim that businessman James W. Bath was hired by the bin Ladens to invest their money and when George W. Bush founded Arbusto Oil, "some $50,000—or 5% of control of Arbusto—came from Mr. Bath." Journalist Craig Unger, who has been critical of the Bush family, discounts this claim, noting that Bath avowed the $50,000 was his own investment, and that Unger himself could find no evidence to the contrary.

Not to mention that Moore's definition of *ties* is insanely loose. Investing in the same company, an action akin to putting your money in the same bank, constitutes ties; but more on that later.

GEORGE W. BUSH ALLOWED BIN LADEN RELATIVES TO LEAVE THE COUNTRY AFTER 9/11

The next theme that takes shape in *Fahrenheit* is Moore's often-repeated assertions that President Bush allowed the bin Laden family to leave the United States immediately after September 11, when the nation's airliners were still grounded. It's a testament to the mob mentality complicit in the success of most conspiracy theories that this little notion has survived for so long, considering how easy it is to disprove.

In *Dude, Where's My Country?*, Moore quotes a *New York Times* article: "The story began: 'In the first days after the terror attacks on New York and Washington, Saudi Arabia supervised the urgent evacuation of 24 members of Osama bin Laden's extended family from the United States. . . .'"

From that short excerpt, Moore spins a complete theory: "[W]hile thousands were stranded and could not fly, if you could prove you were a close relative of the biggest mass-murderer in U.S. history, you get a free trip to gay Paree!" Moore continues, playing on the country's emotions of the events: "A frightened nation struggled to get through those days after September 11. Yet, in the sky above us, the bin Ladens and Saudi royals jetted home. I think we deserve an explanation."

In a February 2002 *Playboy* interview, Moore improved on the tale: "Bush said, No, you're not to interrogate any of the bin Ladens. They get a free pass out of the country. 280 million Americans, and the only people who flew on those three days were people named bin Laden."

Mike has to count on readers not looking up the *New York Times* story he quotes because he made a major deletion. In the very next paragraph, the article he uses as his primary source states that the aircraft carrying the Saudis was "caught up in the FBI dragnet." According to the *Times* article, "Both planes, one Jumbo jet carrying 100 family members, and the other 40, were eventually allowed to leave when airports reopened and passports were checked."

So much for them getting "a free trip to gay Paree" or jetting home while the airports were closed.

Since the *Times* story, more proof has surfaced to undermine Moore's rendition of the facts. Once again, it's Bush family critic Craig Unger weighing in with a timeline that contradicts Moore's past statements.

In his book *House of Bush, House of Saud,* which is unfriendly to President Bush, Unger describes how on September 13 a private plane picked up Saudis (no bin Laden is mentioned) and brought them to checkpoints within the United States. (Actually, whether the flight actually occurred on September 13 is still disputed. Dan Grossi, who served as bodyguard to the Saudis, says it did, but the FBI and the FAA both deny it.) One day later, the Federal Aviation Administration (FAA) cleared private planes to begin flying, which would've been a perfectly legal date for the Saudis to fly anywhere of their choosing.

It wasn't until more than a week later—on September 22—that planes carrying the bin Ladens left the country. (There had been two previous flights: one on September 15 carrying thirteen Saudis and two Britons to London and one on September 16 carrying seven Saudis, most of them with diplomatic status, to Geneva. Manifests obtained by Unger indicate that neither flight carried a bin Laden.)

— 143 —

The 9/11 Commission Report takes Moore to pieces on this:

> First, we found no evidence that any flights of Saudi nationals, domestic or international, took place before the reopening of national airspace on the morning of September 13, 2001. To the contrary, every flight we have identified occurred after national airspace reopened.
>
> Second, we found no evidence of any political intervention. [Discussion follows of how decision was made by Richard Clarke in coordination with the FBI].
>
> Third, we believe that the FBI conducted a satisfactory screening of Saudi nationals who left the United States on charter flights. [Discussion of screening process]. The FBI interviewed all persons of interest on these flights prior to their departures. They concluded that none of the passengers was connected to the 9/11 attacks and have since found no evidence to change that conclusion.

If that weren't enough, Richard Clarke, who is critical of Bush and whom *Fahrenheit* portrays as something of a hero, put in his bit. "I take responsibility for it. I don't think it was a mistake, and I'd do it again," he told the Washington newspaper *The Hill*. "It didn't get any higher than me . . . On 9/11, 9/12, and 9/13, many things didn't get any higher than me. I decided it in consultation with the FBI." He told Associated Press the same thing, adding: "After 9/11, I think the Saudis were perfectly justified . . . in fearing the possibility of vigilantism against Saudis in this country."

When the *Washington Post* contacted Moore for clarification (if that is the right word) of his claims—which formed a major part of *Fahrenheit*'s thesis—he was driven to instant retreat.

While he would not speak for himself, his spokesman told the *Post* that "Moore did not intend to suggest that the bin Ladens flew away while civilian flights were grounded." How this can be reconciled with his quite specific statements in print, while promoting the movie, that the bin Ladens were being flown to "gay Paree" while the rest of us were grounded is not very clear.

In short, this was hardly a suppressed scandal. After 9/11, the national mood turned very ugly toward people wearing Arabic dress and with Arabic names. The Saudis involved included royalty, diplomats, and children of Saudi cabinet ministers. Besides the humanitarian concern, it was also abundantly clear that the United States would need Saudi Arabia as an ally in the struggles to come—and that this alliance would be jeopardized if any Saudis were killed. Getting these individuals out of the country safely would have been a priority for any president with a speck of foresight.

GEORGE W. BUSH IS SECRETLY TIED TO THE CARLYLE GROUP

Fahrenheit reveals another huge scoop here: A quick Google search only turns up 32,400 hits on variations of this story, which has been floating around since the first President Bush was in office.

The Carlyle Group—an international investment firm—is one big business, managing an estimated $18 billion worth of private equity. Carlyle's board is comprised of several former government officials, at least three of whom worked with the first President Bush when he served as CIA director and vice president. Not terribly surprising, then, that the Bush family would have investments there—and certainly no state secret.

But, responds Moore, the bin Laden family also invested $2 million in Carlyle funds. Moore's headline is now clear: Relatives of bin Laden and relatives of Bush have invested in the same fund, proving the linkage between the president and Osama bin Laden!

Unfortunately for Mike's breathtaking thesis, the Bushes and bin Ladens are not the only ones tied in to Carlyle. The two families have a fellow investor in George Soros, the same billionaire financier who is now bankrolling the far-left and anti-Bush organization moveon.org, which is leading much of the Democratic Party's massive soft-money fund-raising initiatives in the 2004 election cycle.

As the *Guardian* notes: "As the Carlyle Group expanded, success brought more investors, including the international financier George Soros and, in 1995, the wealthy Saudi bin Ladin family. . . ."

What's more, some reports have placed Soros' investment in Carlyle at more than $100,000,000—that's *one hundred million dollars*—far dwarfing that of the Bushes and, for that matter, the bin Ladens.

So, we might wonder, why didn't Moore give George Soros at least a cameo in his movie indicting him as yet another tainted partner of the bin Ladens? It's no less a stretch than Moore's other claims—which doesn't mean it isn't completely absurd.

THE GENEVA CONVENTION AS APPLIED TO UNCONSCIOUS DRUNKS

While *Fahrenheit* was in final production, the hot news topic became the treatment of Iraqi detainees at Abu Ghraib prison. Unable to resist a chance for publicity, Moore immediately issued public claims that he had sensational footage of prison abuses and was troubled in conscience because he hadn't revealed it earlier. "I had it months before the story broke on *60 Minutes,* and I really struggled with what to do with it," Moore told the *San Francisco Chronicle.* He added that he feared he'd be accused of seeking publicity for his movie (what? Moore?). "That prevented me from making maybe the right decision." His concern about being accused of publicity-seeking did not stop him from adding, "The stuff with the detainees in my movie is even more shocking than what we saw in that prison . . ."

As a further teaser, Moore told the *New York Times* that he was considering relenting and offering a sneak peak at his shocking atrocity footage: "Mr. Moore said he was considering making at least one sequence from the film available to the news media today after he presents it at the Cannes film festival: that of American soldiers laughing and taking pictures as they place hoods over Iraqi detainees, with one of them touching a prisoner's genitals through a blanket."

When *Fahrenheit* appeared, its supposedly shocking abuse footage consisted of a bunch of detainees, with hoods over their heads, being photographed by soldiers. This was followed by footage that showed an Iraqi, eyes closed and not moving, lying on a stretcher covered by a blanket. One young soldier tickles his feet, and he does not react. Another observes that, "Ali Babba still has a hard-on" and moves as if to poke at it, whereupon the others shout, "You touched his dick!"

Not exactly Buchenwald, or the Japanese POW camps, but some viewers saw the prostrate Iraqi as a corpse, and the actions of the soldiers as callous ridicule of a corpse. When questioned by Liam Lacey of the Canadian *Globe and Mail,* however, Moore had to concede the corpse was not a corpse. In fact, it wasn't even a detainee. Moore "revealed that a scene in which American soldiers appear to be desecrating a corpse beneath a blanket may be misleading. In fact, the soldiers had picked up an old man who had passed out drunk and they poked at his visible erection, covered by a blanket."

Note to Mike: Passed-out drunks are not protected by the Geneva Convention. And one of the occupational hazards of being a passed-out drunk is being ridiculed by passing teenagers, even if one does not display a visible erection. They had at least been nice enough to pick him up off the ground, pop him on a stretcher, and put a blanket over him to keep him warm. If tickling feet and off-color jokes are the worst war atrocity footage that you can find, you'd better stick to filming General Motors.

(The press coverage of Moore's revelation tells us something of the American media's tendency to give Moore a pass when veracity comes up. His revelation was covered by the Canadian newspapers and by BBC News, back in May 2004. While *Fahrenheit*, and its supposed atrocity scene, received extensive coverage in the American press thereafter, we could find not a single article mentioning the deception).

THE BUSH ADMINISTRATION LET BIN LADEN SLIP AWAY

Fahrenheit 9/11 actually did play a modest role in the 2004 election. The movie claimed that the Bush administration actually did not seem too interested in capturing bin Laden; it had gone into Afghanistan with only 11,000 men, and was slow to take the Tora Bora area where bin Laden was rumored to be located. "For all his tough talk, Bush really didn't do much," Moore intones.

After bin Laden released his pre-election videotape, showing that he was still alive (and, ominously for John Kerry, attacking President Bush—which came unpleasantly close to endorsing John Kerry), Kerry seized upon this *Fahrenheit* theme for a comeback. "You want to talk about the war on terror, Mr. President? Let's talk about it," he shouted to supporters. "Let's talk about what happened when you let Osama bin Laden escape in Afghanistan."

Kerry proclaimed that Bush had had bin Laden "cornered in the mountains of Tora Bora," but "outsourced the job of capturing him" to "Afghan warlords who only one week earlier were fighting against us."

If Senator Kerry had only read the first edition of this book, he would have known the risks of swiping arguments from Michael Moore. General Tommy Franks, the career soldier who commanded our forces in Afghanistan, immediately went public with an excoriating response. Franks charged that "the senator's understanding of events doesn't square with reality." He pointed out that no one was certain whether bin Laden even was in Tora Bora; some reports put him in Pakistan or in Kashmir. As far as "outsourcing" went, our Afghan allies knew the difficult mountains of the area, so Special Forces units cooperated with the Afghans to root the Taliban out.

As other reporters picked up the story, it became apparent that the fighting at Tora Bora was not a story of military failure but rather one of adaptation and success. The Afghans had provided the "grunts," and the Special Forces details— riding horses or marching beside them—called in air support and targeted smart bombs on the Taliban caves. Fighting from those mountains and caves, the Afghans had earlier held off the Soviet Army for year after bloody year. Not this time. "Hundreds of al Qaeda fighters died," Melanie Kirk-patrick wrote in the *Wall Street Journal*. "No American life was lost."

THE OVERTHROW OF THE TALIBAN HAD NOTHING TO DO WITH 9/11—IT WAS BUSH'S PLOT TO GET A GAS PIPELINE BUILT

In *Dude, Where's My Country?*, Moore unveils what he sees as a plot: The Afghan invasion and overthrow of the Taliban wasn't purely a reaction to the events of 9/11, but rather had a lot to do with getting an oil pipeline built.

The gist of Moore's argument is that some former Soviet republics have major untapped oil supplies, and to get at them, there exist two competing plans: Unocal's plan to run the pipelines through Afghanistan vs. Enron's plan to run the pipelines under the Caspian Sea. Although the Unocal idea would have put lots of money in the Taliban's pockets, "even President Clinton was all for the idea of the Unocal pipeline."

George W. Bush, then governor of Texas, backed the Enron plan. Then in 1998, President Clinton responded to some terrorist attacks by firing cruise missiles at an empty camp in Afghanistan. Unocal thereupon shelved its Afghan plans. Then followed the election, 9/11, the overthrow of the Taliban, and in late 2001 the new Afghan government signed a deal to permit the pipeline.

An interesting tale . . . but how do you fit a George W. Bush conspiracy theory into it? After all, Bush had backed the Enron plan, which put the pipes under the Caspian and avoided Afghanistan. Clinton was the one backing the rival Unocal plan to put them through Afghanistan.

Moore solves his problem by mixing up the two pipelines (as any reader would, unless the details were outlined). First, he discusses that Taliban representatives were in the United States in 1997 and 1998, the latter trip "sponsored by Clinton's State Department," and met with Unocal in Texas. Moore continues: "In late 1996, Unocal had begun looking into including Uzbekistan in its pipeline deal heading through Afghanistan and into Pakistan." Keep in mind that this is Unocal, sponsored by Clinton officials. Moore charges: "And then you, Mr. Bush, decided to get in on the action. You met personally with Uzbekistan's ambassador on behalf of Enron."

Wait a minute. Moore just switched companies, charging Bush, not with supporting Unocal and its Afghan pipeline but with supporting Enron, which didn't plan an Afghan route!

Having hit his stride, Moore continued: "What role exactly did you play in the Unocal meetings with the Taliban? I'm guessing you knew that the leaders of a foreign country were visiting your state and meeting with people who were donors to your campaign." Again, the sleight of hand. Bush was backing the other pipeline, not this one. And foreign representatives don't need a governor's permission to enter a state—though they did need the Clinton Administration's okay to come here. Moore caps it with, "So why exactly were brutal dictators being wined and dined in your state when you seem to be so against brutal dictators?"

Bush was intervening in support of the *Enron* plan—which meant NO Afghan pipeline and NO money to the Taliban. The people who were touting the Unocal-Taliban deal, with its wining and dining of brutal dictators were . . . the Clinton Administration.

Conspiracy theories aren't hard work. To demonstrate, we'll take a crack at our own—admittedly, it's a bit half-baked, but it's using Moore's oven and recipe. Let's probe the shadowy connections between bin Laden and Michael Moore himself.

1. *Fahrenheit 9/11* was being underwritten by Miramax, to the tune of several million dollars. As Moore wrote in May of 2004, "For the next year, six million dollars of Disney money continued to flow into the production of making my movie."

2. Miramax is a subsidiary of the Disney empire.

3. While Disney derives a lot of its income from Disney sweatshops in third world countries, that's not its only source of financing. It needed serious capital—billions—for its expansion into Euro Disney and to bail out that project when it started to tank.

And guess with whom Disney hopped into bed at that point?

To start with, none other than the Carlyle Group, with (Moore tells us) its bin Laden monies. With the help of its 'access capitalists' such as Baker and Saudi Prince al-Waleed bin Talal (keep that name in mind), Carlyle made deals in the Middle East and Western Europe, including a bailout of Euro Disney, throughout the mid-1990s.

Carlyle Group, Soros, and Prince Talal were not the only ones bailing out Euro Disney. Prince al-Waleed Bin Talal (we told you to keep that name in mind) invested half a billion, and wound up owning 24 percent of the park.

The Euro Disney buyout is not the only link between Disney and these shadowy forces. In 2000, Prince Talal pumped $50,000,000 into Disney itself. Disney is now turning to him for a second bailout.

Start the ominous music. . . ,

The bin Ladens' co-investor in the Carlyle Group, George Soros, suddenly invests as much as *$15 million* in the election, funding moveon.org and other anti-Bush efforts. . . .

Bin Laden–tainted money goes to the Carlyle Group, and they and sundry other Middle Eastern types wind up bankrolling Disney. . . .

Disney's Miramax bankrolls a producer who has produced works that are the standard primers for anti-Americanism today.

And finally, Disney does Moore's film one last, great, favor. A few days before the Cannes Film Festival, Moore announces that Disney has told Miramax it can't distribute his film after all. Moore, of course, trumpets this decision as corporate censorship, designed to prevent Americans from seeing the movie, and in so doing, secures a publicity godsend that millions could not buy.

The owners of Miramax announce that they'll simply form a separate company, buy the rights back off Miramax, and distribute the film.

Later, Moore lets it slip on CNN that he'd been told nearly a year before that Miramax would not be his American distributor—which means that unless he'd somehow forgotten for all that time that he didn't have a distributor, all had been arranged in advance. Within a few days Miramax's owners announced they were negotiating to buy rights to the film so they could distribute it separately from the company.

The multi-million dollar negotiations seem to have gone very quickly: Why, *CNN News* reported that the negotiations were over a day before the *Washington Post* broke the story that they'd begun.

What seems on the surface to be censorship looks more like a remarkably successful publicity stunt, with Disney in effect boosting *Fahrenheit 9/11* on the eve of Cannes, and still standing to make a tidy profit off selling the rights to the new distributor. A nice present from a company which, according to Moore, has ties to Osama. And using Moore's own formula for guilt by association . . .

Gasp! Michael Moore has ties to Osama bin Laden? We can give the answer Moore often gives, when challenged to prove a ridiculous conspiracy theory or baseless personal attack: Maybe not, but these are questions that people should be asking.

With a camera, a microphone, and sufficient cash, you, too, can craft your own version of the world and emblazon it with a premium of fear over facts. Be warned though: Paranoid schizophrenia makes for compelling film, but it's no way of life.

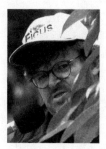

THE FIFTY-NINE DECEITS
OF *FAHRENHEIT 9/11*

David Kopel

I n this report, I number Moore's deceits. Some are omissions that create a false impression; others involve different forms of deception. A few are false statements Moore has made when defending the film. Judge for yourself the credibility of Michael Moore's promise, "Every single fact I state in *Fahrenheit 9/11* is the absolute and irrefutable truth . . . Do

This chapter is excerpted from David Kopel's Web report on *Fahrenheit 9/11*, online at http://www.davekopel.com/Terror/Fiftysix-Deceits-in-Fahrenheit-911.htm. The report has been edited to focus on the most significant deceits identified by Mr. Kopel and to "translate" it from standard webpage layout into a printed form. Additional citations and extended discussions of the issues in this chapter can be found in the Web report, which began as "The Fifty-Six Deceits of *Fahrenheit 9/11*"—the title changed as readers alerted the author to additional Moore deceptions.

Mr. Kopel is a former Assistant Attorney General for the State of Colorado. He is presently the research director of the Independence Institute.

not let anyone say this or that isn't true. If they say that, they are lying."

2000 ELECTION NIGHT

Fahrenheit 9/11 begins on election night 2000. We are first shown Al Gore rocking on stage with famous musicians and a high-spirited crowd. The conspicuous sign on stage reads "Florida Victory." Moore creates the impression that Gore was celebrating his victory in Florida. Moore's voiceover claims, "And little Stevie Wonder, he seemed so happy, like a miracle had taken place." The verb tense of past perfect ("had taken") furthers the impression that the election has been completed.

Actually, the rally took place in the early hours of Election Day, before polls had even opened. Gore did campaign in Florida on Election Day, but went home to Tennessee to await the results. The "Florida Victory" sign reflected Gore's hopes, not any actual election results, as confirmed by the November 7, 2000, *Associated Press* article "Gore Campaigns into Election Day."

The film shows CBS and CNN calling Florida for Al Gore. According to the narrator, "Then something called the Fox News Channel called the election in favor of the other guy? All of a sudden the other networks said, 'Hey, if Fox said it, it must be true.'" We then see NBC anchor Tom Brokaw stating, "All of us networks made a mistake and projected Florida in the Al Gore column. It was our mistake."

Moore thus creates the false impression that the networks withdrew their claim about Gore winning Florida when they heard that Fox said that Bush won Florida.

In fact, the networks that called Florida for Gore did so early in the evening before polls had even closed in the

Florida panhandle, which is part of the Central Time Zone. NBC called Florida for Gore at 7:49 P.M., Eastern Time. This was 10 minutes before polls closed in the Florida panhandle. Thirty seconds later, CBS called Florida for Gore. And at 7:52 P.M., Fox called Florida for Gore. Moore never lets the audience know that *Fox was among the networks that made the error of prematurely calling Florida for Gore.* Then at 8:02 P.M., ABC called Florida for Gore. Only ABC had waited until the Florida polls were closed.

About an hour before the polls closed in panhandle Florida, the networks called the U.S. Senate race in favor of the Democratic candidate. The networks seriously compounded the problem because from 6 to 7 Central Time, they repeatedly announced that polls had closed in Florida—even though polls were open in the panhandle.

The false announcements that the polls were closed, as well as the premature calls (the Presidential race ten minutes early; the Senate race an hour early), may have cost Bush thousands of votes from the conservative panhandle, as discouraged last-minute voters heard that their state had already been decided; some last-minute voters on their way to the polling place turned around and went home. Other voters who were waiting in line left the polling place. Even if the premature television calls affected all potential voters equally, the effect was to reduce Republican votes significantly, because the Florida panhandle is a Republican stronghold. A 2001 study by statistician John Lott suggested that the early calls cost Bush at least 7,500 votes, and perhaps many more. Another study reported that the networks reduced panhandle turnout by about 19,000 votes, costing Bush about 12,000 votes and Gore about 7,000 votes.

At 10:00 P.M., which networks took the lead in retracting the premature Florida win for Gore? They were CNN and CBS, not Fox. (The two networks were using a shared Decision Team.)

In fact, Fox did not retract its claim that Gore had won Florida until 2 A.M.—*four hours after* other networks had withdrawn the call.

Moore's editing technique of the election night segment is typical of his style: all the video clips are real clips, and nothing he says is, narrowly speaking, false. But notice how he says, "Then something called the Fox News Channel called the election in favor of the other guy?" The impression created is that the Fox call of Florida for Bush came soon after the CBS/CNN calls of Florida for Gore, and that Fox caused the other networks to change ("All of a sudden the other networks said, 'Hey, if Fox said it, it must be true.'")

This is the essence of the Moore technique: cleverly blending half-truths which deceive the viewer.

2000 ELECTION RECOUNT

How did Bush win Florida? "Second, make sure the chairman of your campaign is also the vote count woman." Actually, Florida Secretary of State Katherine Harris (who was Bush's Florida co-chair, not "the chairman") was not the "vote count woman." Vote counting in Florida is performed by the election commissioners in each of Florida's counties. The Florida Secretary of State merely certifies the reported vote. The office does not count votes.

A little while later, *Fahrenheit* shows Jeffrey Toobin (a sometime talking-head lawyer for CNN) claiming that if the

Supreme Court had allowed a third recount to proceed past the legal deadline, "under every scenario Gore won the election."

Fahrenheit shows only a snippet of Toobin's remarks on CNN. What *Fahrenheit* does not show is that Toobin admitted on CNN that the only scenarios for a Gore victory involved a type of recount that Gore had never requested in his lawsuits and that would have been in violation of Florida law. Toobin's theory likewise depends on re-assigning votes that are plainly marked for one candidate (Pat Buchanan) to Gore, although there are no provisions in Florida law to guess at whom a voter "really" meant to vote for and to re-assign the vote.

As *USA Today* summarized, on May 11, 2001: "Who would have won if Al Gore had gotten manual counts he requested in four counties? Answer: George W. Bush." It added that Bush would also have won, under three of four possible standards, if the hand recount of "undervotes" had gone ahead, and under the two most widely used standards if both "undervotes" and "overvotes" were hand counted. (Undervotes and overvotes were ballots not counted by the machine because it saw, respectively, either no ballot punch for the Presidential race or else saw two or more. Gore was seeking additional recounts only of undervotes. The only scenarios by which Gore would have won Florida would have involved recounts of "overvotes," and then only if the overvotes were assessed by the less-used standards.)

Moore amplifies the deceit with a montage of newspaper headlines, purporting to show that Gore really won. One article shows a date of December 19, 2001, with a large headline reading, "Latest Florida recount shows Gore won election." The article supposedly comes from the *Pantagraph*, a daily newspaper in Bloomington, Illinois. But actually, the headline is merely for a letter to the editor—not a news article. The letter to the editor headline is significantly enlarged to make it look like an article headline. The actual printed letter looked nothing like the "article" Moore portrayed for the film. The letter ran on December 5, not December 19. The *Pantagraph* contacted Moore's office to ask for an explanation, but the office refused to comment.

BUSH PRESIDENCY BEFORE SEPTEMBER 11

The movie lauds an anti-Bush demonstration that took place in Washington, D.C., on the day of Bush's inauguration. According to Moore, "No President had ever witnessed such a thing on his inauguration day." According to CNN, Richard Nixon faced comparable protests in 1969 and 1973. According to *USA Today*, the anti-Bush organizers claimed that they expected 20,000 protesters to show up, whereas the anti-Nixon protest in 1973 drew 60,000 people.

Moore says, "The plan to have Bush get out of the limo for the traditional walk to the White House was scrapped." But according to the BBC, "Mr. Bush delighted his supporters by getting out of his limousine and walked the last block of the parade, holding hands with his wife Laura."

Near the end of the movie, Bush speaks to a tuxedoed audience. He says, "I call you the haves and the have-mores. Some call you the elite; I call you my base." The joke follows several segments in which Bush is accused of having started the Iraq War in order to enrich business. As far the movie audience can tell, Bush is speaking to some unknown group of rich people. The speech actually comes from the October 19, 2000, Alfred E. Smith Memorial Foundation Dinner. The

2000 event was the 55th annual dinner, which raises money for Catholic hospital charities in New York City. Candidates Bush and Gore were the co-guests of honor at the event, where speakers traditionally make fun of themselves.

Gore joked, "The Al Smith Dinner represents a hallowed and important tradition, which I actually did invent." Lampooning his promise to put Social Security in a "lock box," Gore promised that he would put "Medicare in a walk-in closet," put NASA funding in a "hermetically sealed Ziploc bag" and would "always keep lettuce in the crisper." So although *Fahrenheit* presents the joke as epitomizing Bush's selfishness, the joke really was part of Bush helping to raise $1.6 million for medical care for the poor.

BUSH VACATIONS

Fahrenheit 9/11 states, "In his first eight months in office before September 11th, George W. Bush was on vacation, according to the *Washington Post*, 42 percent of the time." As Tom McNamee of the *Chicago Sun-Times* has noted:

> Shortly before 9/11, the *Post* calculated that Bush had spent forty-two percent of his presidency at vacation spots or en route, including all or part of fifty-four days at his ranch. That calculation, however, includes weekends, which Moore failed to mention.

Many of those days are weekends, and the Camp David stays have included working visits with foreign leaders. Since the Eisenhower administration, presidents have usually spent many weekends at Camp David, which is fully equipped for presidential work. Once the Camp David time is excluded,

Bush's "vacation" time drops to 13 percent. Much of that 13 percent was spent on Bush's ranch in Texas.

Having shown a clip from August 25 with Bush explaining how he likes to work on the ranch, Moore announces "George Bush spent the rest of August at the ranch." Reader Scott Marquardt looked into this August 2001 "vacation." Using public documents from www.whitehouse.gov, here is what he found for the period surrounding August 25:

Friday, August 24

Officials arrived from Washington at 10:00 A.M. Shortly thereafter, at a press conference, Bush announced that General Richard B. Myers will be the Chairman of the Joint Chiefs and General Pete Pac will serve as Vice Chairman of the Joint Chiefs. He also announced fourteen other appointments, and his intentions for the budget. At 11:30 A.M., these officials, as well as National Security Council experts, the Secretary of Defense, and others, met with Bush to continue the strategic review process for military transformation (previous meetings had been held at the Pentagon and the White House). The meeting ended at 5:15.

Met with Andy Card and Karen Hughes, talking about communications issues.

Issued a proclamation honoring Women's Equality Day.

Saturday, August 25

Awoke at 5:45 A.M., read daily briefs.

Had an hour-long CIA and national security briefing at 7:45.

Gave his weekly radio address on the topic of the Budget.

Sunday, August 26

Spoke at the Little League World Series in Williamsport, Pennsylvania.

Spoke at the U.S. Steel Group Steelworkers Picnic at Mon Valley Works, southeast of Pittsburgh. He also visited some employees still working, not at the picnic.

Over the next three days, Bush declared a disaster area in Ohio and ordered federal aid for it, reported to the House on progress toward a "solution of the Cyprus question," announced his nomination for head of the Bureau of Land Management, appointed thirteen members to the Presidential Task Force to Improve Health Care Delivery for Our Nation's Veterans, and addressed the American Legion's annual convention.

By way of underscoring his image of Bush as goofing off, Moore then shows a clip of the president making a statement condemning terrorism, and then hitting a golf ball after quipping "Now watch this drive." This sequence is also taken out of context. The viewer is left with the impression that Bush is referring to al Qaeda, or terrorism in general. The real context: Bush was asked for his reaction to a report of a Palestinian suicide bomber strike against Israel.

(Anyone wishing to object that Bush should have shown more reaction to the event in Israel should note that, according to Bill Clinton's autobiography *My Life*, when President Clinton learned that Israel's Prime Minister, Yitzhak Rabin, had been shot, Clinton went out to the White House lawn and hit golf balls while he waited to learn if Rabin would live. That Clinton played golf after learning of a terrible crime in Israel obviously does not mean that he did not care about the crime.)

Moore wraps up the vacation segment: "It was a summer to remember. And when it was over, he left Texas for his second favorite place." The movie then shows Bush in Florida. Actually, he went back to Washington, where he gave a speech on August 31.

SEPTEMBER 11

Fahrenheit presents a powerful segment on the September 11 attacks. There is no narration, and the music is dramatic yet tasteful. The visuals are reaction shots from pedestrians, as they gasp with horrified astonishment.

Moore has been criticized for using the reaction shots as a clever way to avoid showing the planes hitting the buildings and some of the victims falling to their deaths. Even if this is true, the segment still effectively evokes the horror and outrage that every decent human being still feels about September 11.

But as New York's former Mayor Edward Koch reported, Moore says, "I don't know why we are making so much of an act of terror. It is three times more likely that you will be struck by lightning than die from an act of terror." Moore's first public comment about the September 11 attacks was to complain that too many Democrats rather than Republicans had been killed: "If someone did this to get back at Bush, then they did so by killing thousands of people who did not vote for him! Boston, New York, D.C., and the plane's destination of California—these were places that voted against Bush!" (The quote was originally posted as a "Mike's Message" on Moore's website on September 12, but was removed not long after. Among the many places where Moore's quote has been repeated is the *New Statesman*, a leftist British political magazine.)

A person might feel great personal sympathy for the victim of a lightning strike, but the same person might feel that, overall, the "lightning problem" is not worth making a big fuss over. *Fahrenheit* presents September 11 as a terrible tragedy (in which Moore lost one a professional colleague, and many other people lost loved ones), and as something worth making a big fuss over. On this latter point, *Fahrenheit's* purported view does not appear to be the same as Moore's actual view.

BUSH ON SEPTEMBER 11

Fahrenheit mocks President Bush for continuing to read the book *My Pet Goat* to a classroom of elementary school children after he was told about the September 11 attacks. Actually, as reported in the *New Yorker,* the book he was reading with the class was *Reading Mastery 2*, which contains an exercise called "The Pet Goat." The title of the book is not very important in itself, but the invented title of "My Pet Goat" makes it easier to ridicule Bush.

What Moore did not tell you:

As detailed by the *Washington Times,* Ari Fleischer was in the back of the classroom, holding up a legal pad with the words, "DON'T SAY ANYTHING YET." Bush can be seen looking up and nodding in apparent acknowledgment. The information was still flowing in. It was too early for action or a statement that might commit us to action.

According to the 9/11 Commission staff report, Bush wrapped up his reading, and "He then returned to a holding room shortly before 9:15, where he was briefed by staff and saw television coverage. He next spoke to Vice

President Cheney, Dr. Rice, New York Governor George Pataki, and FBI Director Robert Mueller. He decided to make a brief statement from the school before leaving for the airport."

President Bush knew he was on camera, and it would be reasonable to expect that if he had suddenly sped out of the room, his hasty movement would have been replayed incessantly on television; leaving the room quickly might have exacerbated the national mood of panic, even if Bush had excused himself calmly. The Secret Service may well have been cautious about moving Bush, not only because of hijackings, but also because on the morning of September 11, a Middle Eastern man had tried to gain personal access to the president by falsely claiming that he was a journalist with a scheduled interview, and by asking for a Secret Service agent by name.

Bush's reaction was praised by a witness with a front-row seat. Gwendolyn Tose-Rigell, the principal of Emma E. Booker Elementary School. "I don't think anyone could have handled it better," she told the *Associated Press*. "What would it have served if he had jumped out of his chair and ran out of the room?" She added that Bush's presence had a calming effect and "helped us get through a very difficult day."

Moore does not offer any suggestion about what the president should have done during those few minutes, rather than staying calm for the sake of the classroom and of the public. Nor does Moore point to any way that the September 11 events might have turned out better in even the slightest way if the president had acted differently. I agree with Lee Hamilton, the vice-chair of the September 11 Commission and a former Democratic Representative from Indiana: "Bush made the right decision in remaining calm, in not rushing out of the classroom."

PRE-9/11 BRIEFING

Castigating the allegedly lazy president, Moore says, "Or perhaps he just should have read the security briefing that was given to him on August 6, 2001, that said that Osama bin Laden was planning to attack America by hijacking airplanes."

Moore supplies no evidence for his implication that President Bush did not read the August 6, 2001, Presidential Daily Brief.

Moore smirks that perhaps President Bush did not read the briefing because its title was so vague. Moore then cuts to Condoleezza Rice announcing the title of the briefing: "Bin Laden Determined to Strike in U.S." Here, Moore seems to be playing off Condoleezza Rice's testimony of the September 11 Commission that the contents of the memo were vague.

However, no one (except Moore) has ever claimed that Bush did not read the briefing, or that he did not read it because the title was vague. Rather, Condoleezza Rice had told the press conference that the *information* in the briefing was "very vague."

The content of the briefing supports Rice's characterization, and refutes Moore's assertion that the briefing "said that Osama bin Laden was planning to attack America by hijacking airplanes." The actual briefing was highly equivocal:

> We have *not been able to corroborate* some of the *more sensational* threat reporting, such as that from a [deleted text] service in 1998 saying that Bin Laden wanted to

hijack a U.S. aircraft to gain the release of "Blind Shaykh" Umar Abd al-Rahman and other U.S.-held extremists.

Nevertheless, FBI information since that time indicates patterns of suspicious activity in this country consistent with preparations for hijackings or other types of attacks, including recent surveillance of federal buildings in New York.

BUSH AND JAMES BATH

Moore mentions that Bush's friend from his National Guard days, James Bath, had become the money manager for the bin Laden family, then adds that "James Bath himself in turn invested in George W. Bush," putting a sum into Bush's energy company, Arbusto. Moore doesn't mention, as reported by MSNBC, the *Weekly Standard,* and *Newsday,* that Bath has said that he had invested his own money, not the bin Ladens', in Bush's company.

Moore makes a big point about the name of James Bath being blacked out from Bush National Guard records that were released by the White House. The blackout might appear less sinister if Moore revealed that federal law (the Health Insurance Portability and Accountability Act, or HIPAA) required the National Guard to black out the names any Guardsmen whose medical information was on the same pages as the records which the Guard released regarding George Bush's health records. In Bath's case, he had been suspended for failing to take an annual physical exam. So what Moore presents as a sinister effort to conceal the identity of James Bath was in fact the legally required compliance with federal law.

Moore gloats: "What Bush didn't know was that I already had a copy of his military records—uncensored—obtained in the year 2000." Moore creates the impression that he is an investigative sleuth. Actually, the records had been released in 2000. The privacy regulations for the Health Insurance Portability and Accountability Act (HIPAA) went into effect on April 14, 2003, and so did not apply when the National Guard records were released in 2000.

BUSH AND PRINCE BANDAR

Moore points out the distressingly close relationship between Saudi Arabia's ambassador, Prince Bandar, and the Bush family. But Moore does not explain that Bandar has been a bipartisan Washington power broker for decades, and that, as documented in the *New Yorker*, Bill Clinton repeatedly relied on Bandar to advance Clinton's own Middle East agenda.

President Clinton's former Ambassador to Saudi Arabia, Wyche Fowler, has been earning a lucrative living as a Saudi apologist and serving as chairman of the Middle East Institute, a research organization heavily funded by Saudi Arabia. Former President Clinton received $750,000 for giving a speech in Saudi Arabia, and the Saudis have donated a secret sum (estimated between $1 million and $20 million) to the Clinton Library.

Former President Carter (who invited Moore to sit in his private box at the 2004 Democratic Convention) met with ten bin Laden brothers in 2000, and came away with a $200,000 donation from the bin Ladens to the Carter Center in Atlanta.

I am not suggesting that Mr. Fowler or former President Carter are in any way corrupt; I'm sure that they are sincere (although, in my view, mistaken) in their pro-Saudi and anti-Israel viewpoint. Nor is there anything illegal about former President Clinton's receipt of huge Saudi largesse. What is misleading is for Moore to look at the web of Saudi influence in Washington only in regard to the Republican Bushes, and to ignore the fact that Saudi influence and money are widespread in both parties.

HARKEN ENERGY

Bush once served on the board of directors of the Harken Energy Company. According to *Fahrenheit:*

> **MOORE:** Yes, it helps to be the president's son. Especially when you're being investigated by the Securities and Exchange Commission.
>
> **TV REPORTER:** In 1990 when Mr. Bush was a director of Harken Energy he received this memo from company lawyers warning directors not to sell stock if they had unfavorable information about the company. One week later he sold $848,000 worth of Harken stock. Two months later, Harken announced losses of more than $23 million dollars.
>
> **MOORE:** Bush beat the rap from the SEC?

What Moore left out: Bush sold the stock long after he checked with those same "company lawyers" who had provided the cautionary memo, and they told him that the sale was all right. Almost all of the information that caused Harken's large quarterly loss developed only after Bush had sold the stock.

Despite Moore's pejorative that Bush "beat the rap," no one has ever found any evidence suggesting that he engaged in illegal insider trading. He did fail to file a particular SEC disclosure form on time. For a detailed factual timeline, see James Dunbar, "A Brief History of Bush, Harken, and the SEC," Center for Public Integrity, October 16, 2002.

CARLYLE GROUP

Moore's film suggests that Bush has close family ties to the bin Laden family, principally through Bush's father's relationship with the Carlyle Group, a private investment firm. The president's father, George H. W. Bush, was a senior adviser to the Carlyle Group's Asian affiliate until recently. Members of the bin Laden family, who own one of Saudi Arabia's biggest construction firms had invested two million dollars in a Carlyle Group fund. (Bush Sr. and the bin Ladens have since severed ties with the Carlyle Group, which in any case has a bipartisan roster of partners, including Bill Clinton's former SEC chairman Arthur Levitt.) The movie quotes author Dan Briody claiming that the Carlyle Group "gained" from September 11 because it owned United Defense, a military contractor.

As Michael Isikoff noted in *Newsweek*, United Defense holds a special distinction among U.S. defense contractors that is not mentioned in Moore's movie: The firm's $11 billion Crusader self-propelled artillery system is one of the few weapons systems *canceled* by the Bush administration.

Moore's website does try to answer this criticism, claiming that refusing to mention the Crusader cancellation was all right because the cancellation came after the United Defense initial public offering (stock sale to the public). But the cancellation had a serious negative financial impact on Carlyle, since Carlyle still owns 47 percent of United Defense.

Moore tells us that when Carlyle took United Defense public, Carlyle made a one-day profit of $237 million, but under all the public scrutiny, the bin Laden family eventually had to withdraw. Moore doesn't tell us that they withdrew before the public offering, not after it.

There is another famous investor in Carlyle whom Moore does not reveal: George Soros. But the fact that the anti-Bush billionaire has invested in Carlyle would detract from Moore's simplistic conspiracy theory.

Moore alleges that the Saudis have given $1.4 billion dollars to the Bushes and their associates. But, as noted by MSNBC, nearly 90 percent of that amount, or $1.18 billion, comes from just one source: military training contracts in the early and mid-1990s between Saudi Arabia and the BDM corporation. BDM's asserted connection with the Bushes is that it was owned for a time by the Carlyle Group, an investment house whose advisory boards include former President George H. Bush. MSNBC's investigation found one problem with this supposed Bush connection: Carlyle Group had sold its interest in BDM five months *before* the elder Bush joined Carlyle's advisory board in 1998, although other Bush associates had joined Carlyle before 1998.

SAUDI INVESTMENTS IN THE UNITED STATES

Moore asks author Craig Unger: "How much money do the Saudis have invested in America, roughly?" Unger replies, "Uh, I've heard figures as high as $860 billion dollars."

What is the basis of Unger's claim? The $860 billion figure appears on page twenty eight of Unger's *House of Bush, House of Saud.* He cites two sources, neither of which supports the $860 billion figure. Unger may have "heard" the figure of $860 billion dollars, but probably from people who were repeating the factoid, which was unsupported in his own book.

Unger is asked: "What percentage of our economy is that?" (Meaning the supposed $860 billion.)

He replies, "Well, in terms of investments on Wall Street, American equities, it's roughly six or seven percent of America. They own a fairly good slice of America." A little bit later, Moore states that "Saudi Prince Bandar is perhaps the best protected ambassador in the U.S. Considering how he and his family, and the Saudi elite own 7 percent of America, it's probably not a bad idea."

According to the Bureau of Economic Analysis, total foreign investment in the United States in 2003 was $10,515 billion dollars. This means that even if the figure that Unger "heard" about Saudis having $860 billion is correct, then the Saudis would only have about 8 percent of total *foreign* investment in the United States. Unless you believe that almost all American assets are owned by foreigners, then it cannot possibly be true that Saudis "own 7 percent of America."

SPECIAL PROTECTION FOR SAUDI EMBASSY

Moore shows himself filming the movie near the Saudi embassy in Washington, D.C., and says "Even though we were nowhere near the White House, for some reason the Secret Service had shown up to ask us what we were doing standing across the street from the Saudi embassy?" He tells a uniformed Secret Service officer that he "didn't realize the Secret Service guards foreign embassies," and the officer replies, "not usually, no sir."

But in fact, as Michigan columnist Debbie Schlussel notes, "Any tourist to Washington, D.C., will see plenty of

Secret Service police guarding all of the other foreign embassies which request such protection. Other than guarding the White House and some federal buildings, it's the largest use of personnel by the Secret Service's Uniformed Division."

According to the Secret Service website:

> Uniformed Division officers provide protection for the White House Complex, the Vice-President's residence, the Main Treasury Building and Annex, and foreign diplomatic missions and embassies in the Washington, D.C., area.

So there is nothing strange about the Secret Service protecting the Saudi embassy in Washington, especially since al Qaeda attacks have taken place against Saudi Arabia. According to Article 22 of the Vienna Convention on Diplomatic Relations, an international agreement that has been ratified by the United States, every host country (including the United States) is obliged to protect every embassy within its borders. The Secret Service Agent's reaction that the Service doesn't "usually" guard embassies is explicable: there are 170 foreign embassies in Washington, D.C., many of which require no particular protection from terror, violent demonstrations or other such threats.

PROPOSED UNOCAL PIPELINE IN AFGHANISTAN

This segment is introduced with the question, "Or was the war in Afghanistan really about something else?" The "something else" is shown to be a Unocal pipeline. Unocal proposed that an oil and gas pipeline system run through Afghanistan, which was then Taliban-controlled. Moore mentions that a Taliban delegation visited Texas while Bush was governor, and suggests that the war in Afghanistan was meant as another way of getting the pipeline built.

The Facts: (1) The pipeline was backed by the Clinton Administration. (2) As governor, Bush never met with the delegation. Clinton administration officials, however, did. (3) Unocal dropped the idea years before the United States attacked the Taliban.

As Matt Labash noted in the *Weekly Standard*, "Moore doesn't say that they never actually met with Bush or that the deal went bust in 1998 and had been supported by the Clinton administration."

"Whatever the motive, the Unocal pipeline project was entirely a Clinton-era proposal," Michael Isikoff and Mark Hosenball report on MSNBC. "By the time George W. Bush took office, it was a dead issue and no longer the subject of any lobbying in Washington."

Moore claims that "Enron stood to benefit from the pipeline." To the contrary, Enron was not part of the consortium that expressed interest in working with Unocal on the pipeline.

On December 9, 2003, the new Afghanistan government did sign a protocol with Turkmenistan and Pakistan to facilitate a pipeline. Indeed, it is likely that any rational Afghani government would rationally seek the revenue that could be gained from a pipeline. But the protocol merely aims to entice corporations to build a new pipeline; no corporation has agreed to do so. Nor does the new proposed pipeline even resemble Unocal's failed proposal. The new pipeline would bring oil and gas from the Caspian Sea basin, whereas Unocal's proposal involved deposits five hundred miles away, in eastern Turkmenistan.

According to *Fahrenheit,* Afghanistan's new president, Hamid Karzai, was a Unocal consultant. The origin of the claim appears to be a December 6, 2001, story in the center-left French newspaper *Le Monde.* The story does not cite any source for its claim. Unocal has denied that Karzai was ever a consultant.

Moore's webpage attempts responses to these issues: Regarding Karzai, it cites the article in *Le Monde,* and two later articles which appear to use *Le Monde*'s information. Moore's translation is: "He was a consultant for the American oil company Unocal, while they studied the construction of a pipeline in Afghanistan." The actual sentence was: "Après Kaboul et l'Inde ou il a étudié le droit, il a parfait sa formation aux Etats-Unis ou il fut un moment consultant de l'enterprise pétrolière américaine Unocal, quand celle-ci étudiant la construction d'un oléduc en Afghanistan." Translated properly, this sentence actually reads: "After Kabul and India where he had studied law, he completed his training in the United States where he was briefly (literally: 'for a moment') a consultant for the American petroleum business Unocal, when it was studying the construction of a pipeline in Afghanistan." Neither *Le Monde* nor Moore has provided any evidence to substantiate the claim about Unocal and Karzai.

Moore does not attempt to defend on his website the other false statements that are detailed in this section: that Unocal had abandoned the project in 1998, that the 2003 Protocol involves an entirely different pipeline, and that the pipeline footage in the movie has nothing to do with either the 1998 or 2003 proposals.

BUSH ADMINISTRATION RELATIONSHIP WITH THE TALIBAN

Moore suggests that the Bush administration tried to cozy up to the Taliban. He cites a March 2001 visit to the United

States by a Taliban envoy, with the comment that the Bush administration "welcomed" the official, Sayed Hashemi, "to tour the United States to help improve the image of the Taliban."

But, as *Newsday* noted, "Hashemi's reception at the State Department was hardly welcoming. The administration rejected his claim that the Taliban had complied with U.S. requests to isolate Osama bin Laden and affirmed its nonrecognition of the Taliban. 'We don't recognize any government in Afghanistan,' State Department spokesman Richard Boucher said on the day of the visit."

REPRESENTATIVE PORTER GOSS

Defending the USA Patriot Act, Representative Porter Goss says that he has an "800 number" for people to call to report problems with the Act. *Fahrenheit* shoots back with a caption, "Not really true." The ordinary telephone number (area code 202) for Goss's office is then flashed on the screen.

You'd never know by watching *Fahrenheit,* but Rep. Goss *does* have a toll-free number to which USA Patriot Act complaints can be reported. The number belongs to the Committee that Goss chairs, the House Permanent Select Committee on Intelligence. The number is (877) 858-9040.

OREGON TROOPERS

There are several scenes involving Oregon state troopers who patrol coastal areas in the state. The troopers are presented as under-funded and spread far too thinly.

But this has nothing to do with *Fahrenheit's* claim that the Bush administration is not sincerely interested in homeland security. The Oregon State Police are paid by the Oregon state government (which has been suffering from a budget crisis).

Moreover, the job of protecting the Oregon coastline from foreign invaders is not a job of the Oregon State Police. That job is the responsibility of the U.S. Coast Guard and the U.S. Navy. For the Oregon-Washington coast, the Coast Guard has 1,287 personnel on active duty, 459 Coast Guard Reserves, and 1,600 volunteer in the Coast Guard Auxiliary.

SADDAM HUSSEIN NEVER MURDERED AMERICANS

Fahrenheit asserts that Saddam's Iraq was a nation that "had never attacked the United States. A nation that had never threatened to attack the United States. A nation that had never murdered a single American citizen." Each of these assertions is false. If the subject were not so serious, the extent to which Moore must parse his phrasing to defend his position would be a source of mirth. Challenged by ABC News' Jake Tapper to defend his position, Moore argued that he had not claimed Hussein's regime had never killed an American, but only that it "did not commit a premeditated murder" of one. Tapper continued, noting that Sadaam had given shelter to Abu Nidal, who had murdered Americans, had funded suicide bombers in Israel, who had killed Americans, and had attempted to blow up former President George H. Bush when he visited Kuwait in 1993. Moore refused to budge: "Nothing you just said is proof that the Iraqi government ever murdered an American citizen."

Actually, Tapper missed a few items of Sadaam's anti-American violence. While in power, he had also given protection to the 1993 World Trade Center bombmaker, Abdul Rahman Yasin. In 1991, he ordered his agents to murder the

American Ambassador to the Philippines and, separately, to murder the employees of the U.S. Information Service in Manila; they tried, but failed. Laurie Mylroie, who was Bill Clinton's Iraq advisor during his 1992 campaign, contends that the ringleader of the 1993 World Trade Center bombing, Ramzi Yousef, was working for the Iraqi intelligence services. Yet none of these aggressions against the United States "count" for Moore, because he has carefully framed his verbs and verb tenses to exclude them.

Also, Saddam's military constantly shot at (and therefore attempted to kill) American and British pilots enforcing the "no-fly zone" over portions of Iraq. The no-fly zone was created to prevent Saddam's air force from being able to mass murder Iraqis; Saddam agreed to the no-fly zone as a condition of the ceasefire in the 1991 Gulf War, but then refused to abide by the ceasefire conditions (As he likewise refused to abide by the conditions requiring him to prove that he had destroyed all his weapons of mass destruction). One could argue about whether it is attempted "murder" to break the terms of a ceasefire and to attempt to kill foreign soldiers who are attempting to prevent you from perpetrating mass murder.

SADDAM'S THREATS

Moore's pro-Saddam allegation that Saddam "never threatened to attack the United States" is true in the narrow sense that Saddam never gave a speech in which he threatened to, for example, send the Iraqi navy and army to conduct an amphibious invasion of Florida. But although Saddam never threatened the territorial integrity of America, he repeatedly threatened Americans. Steven Hayes notes that, on November 15, 1997, the main propaganda organ for the Saddam regime, the newspaper *Babel* (which was run by Saddam Hussein's son Uday) ordered: "American and British interests, embassies, and naval ships in the Arab region should be the targets of military operations and commando attacks by Arab political forces." On November 25, 2000, Saddam declared in a televised speech, "The Arab people have not so far fulfilled their duties. They are called upon to target U.S. and Zionist interests everywhere and target those who protect these interests."

On the first anniversary of the September 11 attacks, a weekly newspaper owned by Uday Hussein said that Arabs should "use all means—and they are numerous—against the aggressors . . . and considering everything American as a military target, including embassies, installations, and American companies, and to create suicide/martyr [fidaiyoon] squads to attack American military and naval bases inside and outside the region, and mine the waterways to prevent the movement of war ships. . . ."

IRAQ AND AL QAEDA

Moore declares that George Bush fabricated an Iraq/al Qaeda connection in order to deflect attention from his Saudi masters. But consider the facts presented in Stephen F. Hayes's book, *The Connection: How al Qaeda's Collaboration with Saddam Hussein Has Endangered America*. Hayes notes numerous contacts and coordination of efforts between Hussein's regime and al Qaeda—the classing of bin Laden as an Iraqi intelligence asset in a captured 1992 document, reports of a non-aggression pact the following year, meetings and telephone negotiations throughout the decade, al Qaeda officials operating under protection in Baghdad.

The preliminary staff report of the September 11 Commission stated, "We have no credible evidence that Iraq and al Qaeda cooperated on attacks against the United States." Some critics, including the chief prosecutor of the World Trade Center bombers, have argued that the staff report inexplicably ignored substantial evidence of Iraqi involvement in the September 11 attacks. The final Commission Report finds that there were "friendly contacts" between al Qaeda and the Saddam regime. The Commission does not find that there was a "collaborative operational relationship" for "carrying out attacks against the United States." Whether you agree with the preliminary staff report, the staff's critics, or the final Commission report, there is no dispute that Saddam Hussein had a relationship with al Qaeda, an organization whose only activity was terrorism. *Fahrenheit* dishonestly pretends that there was no relationship at all.

Fahrenheit shows Condoleezza Rice saying, "Oh, indeed there is a tie between Iraq and what happened on 9/11." The audience laughs derisively. Here is what Rice really said on the CBS Early Show, November 28, 2003:

> Oh, indeed there is a tie between Iraq and what happened on 9/11. *It's not that Saddam Hussein was somehow himself and his regime involved in 9/11, but, if you think about what caused 9/11, it is the rise of ideologies of hatred* that lead people to drive airplanes into buildings in New York . . .

Moore deceptively cut the Rice quote to fool the audience into thinking she was making a particular claim, even though she was pointedly not making such a claim. And since Rice spoke in November 2003, her quote had nothing to do with building up American fears before the March 2003 invasion, although Moore implies otherwise.

IRAQ BEFORE LIBERATION

Moore cunningly sequences "home movies," allegedly from prewar Iraq, showing children flying kites, a happy married couple, and people going about their business, with images of a building being destroyed by American bombs. As Jonathan Foreman noted in the *New York Post:* "What Moore presumably doesn't know, or simply doesn't care about, is that the building you see being blown up is the Iraqi Ministry of Defense in Baghdad. Not many children flew kites there. It was in a part of the city that ordinary Iraqis weren't allowed to visit, on pain of death."

We also have the voice of experience. Iraqi blogger Sarmad Zanga gave his reaction to this sequence:

> Excuse me is this my Baghdad you talk about, that Baghdad I live in for more than 20 year, with all what we lived through, how could we be happy and smiling? . . . I got friends executed, I got b[r]others in jail, how? We can be happy, and we got nothing to eat, how? [W]e can be happy, and we got nothing to live for, Iraq was ruled by a regime that had forced a sixth of its population into fearful exile, maybe you have the answers?

MAJOR GREGORY STONE AND RESERVIST PETER DAMON

In order to create a tragic mood, Moore at one point shows the burial, in Arlington National Cemetery, of U.S. Air Force Major Gregory Stone. Major Stone had been killed by a grenade thrown into his tend by Sgt. Hasan K. Akbar, who is awaiting trial on charges of murder. The footage used by Moore includes Major Stone's fiancé, Tammie Eslinger, kissing her hand and touching it to his coffin.

Where Moore secured the footage is unknown, but he appears to have made no effort to secure the family's consent for its use in his movie. Kandi Gallagher, Major Stone's Aunt, told the *Washington Times* that the family is "furious that Greg was in that casket and cannot defend himself," adding that he would have found *Fahrenheit 9/11* "putrid" if he had lived to see it. Major Stone's mother called Moore "a maggot that eats off the dead."

Fahrenheit shows an interview in Walter Reed Army Medical Center with Massachusetts National Guardsman Peter Damon. Damon lost parts of both his arms in Iraq and is learning how to use prosthetic arms. The footage comes from an interview Damon granted to *NBC Nightly News.* Damon's wife says that he never granted Moore permission to use the footage, was never asked, and strongly objects to being used in the film. It hardly seems ethical for a film-maker who dedicates his film to the soldiers in Iraq to put a double-amputee veteran into the film without even bothering to ask for permission. Damon complained to the *New York Daily News* that "The whole movie makes soldiers look like a bunch of idiots . . . I'm not a child. We sent ourselves over there . . . I agree with the President 100 percent. A lot of the guys down at Walter Reed feel the same way."

SUPPORT FOR SOLDIERS AND VETERANS

Bush "supported closing veterans hospitals" says Moore. The Bush Department of Veterans Affairs did propose closing seven hospitals in areas with declining populations where the hospitals were underutilized, and whose veterans could be served by other hospitals. Moore does not say that the Department also proposed building new hospitals in areas where needs were growing, and also building blind rehabilitation centers and spinal cord injury centers . . .

According to Moore, Bush "tried to double the prescription drug costs for veterans." What Bush proposed was raising the prescription co-pay from $7 to $15, for veterans with incomes of over $24,000 a year. Prescription costs would have remained very heavily subsidized by taxpayers. Some, not all, veterans would have faced a doubling of their prescription co-pay, but only to a level that is common for many people with prescription insurance, and hardly a large enough increase to make a great difference in most cases.

Bush, announces Moore, "proposed cutting combat soldiers' pay by 33 percent"—Not exactly. In addition to regular military salaries, soldiers in certain areas (not just combat zones) receive an "imminent danger" bonus of $150 a month. In April 2003, Congress retroactively enacted a special increase of $75, for the fiscal year of October 1, 2002, through September 30, 2003. At first, the Bush administration did not support renewing the special bonus, but then changed its position.

Likewise, Congress had passed a special one-year increase in the family separation allowance (for service personnel stationed in places where their families cannot join them) from $100 to $250. Bush's initial opposition to extending the special increase was presented by Moore as "cutting assistance to their families by 60 percent."

Even if one characterizes not renewing a special bonus as a "cut," *Fahrenheit* misleads the viewer into thinking that the cuts applied to total compensation, rather than only to pay supplements which constitute a small percentage of a soldier's income. An enlisted man with four months of experience receives an annual salary of more than $27,000. (The figure includes the value of health care, housing, and so on.) So allowing the $75 per month supplemental bonus to expire would have amounted to a "cut" of only about 3 percent of total compensation, even at the lowest levels. So Moore's claim of a "33 percent" cut is a ten-fold exaggeration.

Although Moore presents Bush as cutting military pay, Bush did the opposite. In 2003, Congress enacted a Bush administration proposal to raise all military salaries by 3.7 percent, with extra "targeted" pay increases for noncommissioned officers . . .

CONGRESSIONAL CHILDREN IN WAR

Early in this segment, Moore states that "out of the 535 members of Congress, only one had an enlisted son in Iraq." The action of the segment consists of Moore accosting Congressmen to try to convince them to have their children enlist in the military. At the end, Moore declares, "Not a single member of Congress wanted to sacrifice their child for the war in Iraq."

Moore's second statement is technically true, but duplicitous. Of course no-one would want to "sacrifice" his child in any way. But the fact is, Moore's opening ("only one") and his conclusion ("not a single member") are both incorrect. Sergeant Brooks Johnson, the son of South Dakota Democratic Senator Tim Johnson, serves in the 101st Airborne Division and fought in Iraq in 2003. The son of California Republican Representative Duncan Hunter quit his job after September 11 and enlisted in the Marines; his artillery unit was deployed in the heart of terrorist territory in February 2004. Delaware Senator Joseph Biden's son Beau is on active duty in the Judge Advocate General Corps; although Beau Biden has no control over where he is deployed, he has not been sent to Iraq, and therefore does not "count" for Moore's purposes. Seven members of Congress have been confirmed to have children in the military.

How about Cabinet members? *Fahrenheit* never raises the issue, because the answer would not fit Moore's thesis. Attorney General John Ashcroft's son is serving on the U.S.S. McFaul in the Persian Gulf.

Why not count Duncan Hunter's son? Note the phrasing: "only one had an enlisted son in Iraq." Although Hunter's son "enlisted" in the Marines, he is a Second Lieutenant, which means that he is above the rank of an "enlisted man." But why hide from the viewers how many Congressmen really have sons serving in the military in Iraq?

The editing of the Congressional scenes is likewise deceptive. Representative Mark Kennedy (R-MN) is shown in one scene as Moore approaches him to ask if he would be willing to send his son to Iraq. He appears defensive and bewildered as the film cuts to another scene. Kennedy, however, stated that he had told Moore he had a nephew en route to Afghanistan. He also stated that he offered to take Moore up on his request to petition other lawmakers to ask their sons to enlist.

George Stephanopoulos, of ABC News, asked Moore about the selective cuts in the Kennedy footage, and Moore replied that "Well, at the time, when we interviewed him, he didn't have any family members in Afghanistan." Moore continued (with a miswording of Rep. Kennedy's statement) that "Any time a guy like this comes along and says, 'I told him I had two nephews and one was going to Iraq and one was going to Afghanistan,' he's lying . . . And people can go to my Web site and read the transcript and read the truth. What he just said there, what you just quoted, is not true."

The transcript on Moore's website, however, put the lie to Moore's bluster. In the film, Moore says, "Congressman, I'm trying to get members of Congress to get their kids to enlist in the Army and go over to Iraq." But, from the transcript, here's the rest:

> **MOORE:** Is there any way you could help me with that?
>
> **KENNEDY:** How would I help you?
>
> **MOORE:** Pass it out to other members of Congress.
>
> **KENNEDY:** I'd be happy to—especially those who voted for the war. I have a nephew on his way to Afghanistan.

So while *Fahrenheit* pretended that Kennedy just stupidly looked at Moore, Kennedy agreed to help Moore.

Notice also how Moore phrased his reply to Stephanopoulos: "Any time a guy like this comes along and says, 'I told him I had two nephews and one was going to Iraq and one was going to Afghanistan,' he's lying." But Kennedy never claimed that he had a nephew going to Iraq. The insinuation that Kennedy made such a claim is a pure fabrication by Moore.

Are Congressional children less likely to serve in Iraq than children from other families? Let's use Moore's methodology, and ignore members of extended families (such as nephews) and also ignore service anywhere except Iraq (even though U.S. forces are currently fighting terrorists in many countries). And like Moore, let us also ignore the fact that some families have no children, or no children of military age.

We then see that of 535 Congressional families, there are two with a child who served in Iraq. How does this compare with American families in general? In the summer of 2003, U.S. troop levels in Iraq were raised to 145,000. If we factor in troop rotation, we could estimate that about 300,000 people have served in Iraq at some point. According to the Census Bureau (http://www.census.gov/prod/2001pubs/p20-537.pdf), there were 104,705,000 households in the United States in 2000. (See Table 1 of the Census Report.) So the ratio of ordinary U.S. households to Iraqi service personnel is 104,705,000 to 300,000. This reduces to a ratio of 349:1. In contrast the ratio of Congressional households to Iraqi service personnel is 535:2. This reduces to a ratio of 268:1.

Stated another way, a Congressional household is about 23 percent *more likely* than an ordinary household to be closely related to an Iraqi serviceman or servicewoman.

Moore also ignores the fact that there are 101 veterans currently serving in the House of Representatives and 36 in the Senate. Regardless of whether they have children who could join the military, all of the veterans in Congress have personally put themselves at risk to protect their country.

Moore's website response: He cites a May 11, 2003, article in the *St. Louis Post-Dispatch* that only Brooks Johnson had a son who had fought in Iraq. The article was accurate at the time, since Duncan Hunter's son, who had already enlisted, had not yet been sent to Iraq. But *Fahrenheit* premiered at the Cannes Film Festival in May 2004—two months after it had been reported that Duncan Hunter's son had been sent to Iraq. At the least, Moore could acknowledge that his claim about "only one" child is inaccurate, and blame the error on his having not noticed the news about Hunter while the movie was in its final production stages. But instead,

Moore continues to repeat the "only one" claim, which is indisputably false.

MOORE LENDS SUPPORT TO TERRORISTS

In *Fahrenheit 9/11*, Moore claims to support our troops. But in fact, his words lend support to the enemy in Iraq, the coalition of Saddam loyalists, al Qaeda operatives, and terrorists controlled by Iran or Syria, who are united in their desire to murder Iraqis, and to destroy any possibility of democracy in Iraq. Here is what Moore's webpage says about the forces who are killing Americans and trying to impose totalitarian rule on Iraq: "The Iraqis who have risen up against the occupation are not 'insurgents' or 'terrorists' or 'The Enemy.' They are the REVOLUTION, the Minutemen, and their numbers will grow—and they will win."

Of course, if you believe that the people who are perpetrating suicide bombings against Iraqi civilians and American soldiers for the purpose of forcing a totalitarian boot onto Iraq are the moral equivalent of the American Founders, then Moore's claim about the Iraqi insurgents could be valid. But even if that claim were valid (and I do not believe that any reasonable person can equate people fighting for totalitarianism with people fighting for constitutional democracy), then Moore is still being dishonest in *Fahrenheit* when he pronounces his concern for American troops. To the contrary, he is offering off-the-wall praise to the forces who are killing our troops, as he equates the killers with freedom-fighters. And if you think that the people who are slaughtering American soldiers, American civilians, Iraqi soldiers, and Iraqi civilians are terrorists rather than "Minutemen," then it is true that Moore lends support to terrorists. By the way, the number of Iraqi victims of Moore's "Minutemen" out-numbers American victims by about 10:1.

There are some sincere opponents of the Iraq War who want to "support our troops" by bringing them home, and thereby getting them out danger. But it's deceptive to say that you support the troops if (besides lobbying for troop withdrawal) you are allowing your film to be used as a re-cruiting device in certain Arab countries. Moore is doing so, as the next item details.

TERRORISTS SUPPORT FAHRENHEIT

As reported in the trade journal *Screen Daily*, affiliates of the Iranian and Syrian-backed terrorist group Hezbollah are promoting *Fahrenheit 9/11*, and Moore's Middle East distrib-utor, Front Row, has no moral problems with this.

> In terms of marketing the film, Front Row is getting a boost from organizations related to Hezbollah which have rung up from Lebanon to ask if there is anything they can do to support the film. And although [Front Row's Managing Director Gianluca] Chacra says he and his company feel strongly that *Fahrenheit* is not anti-Ameri-can, but anti-Bush, "we can't go against these organiza-tions as they could strongly boycott the film in Lebanon and Syria."

Salon.com confirmed the story, with the note that "Chacra was unfazed, even excited, about their offer: 'Having the support of such an entity in Lebanon is quite significant for that market and not at all controversial. I think it's quite natural.'"

Screen Daily explained that Moore's film would open in mid-July 2005 on ten screens in Lebanon and two screens in

Syria. Syria is a terrorist state that invaded Lebanon in the 1970s and controls the nation through a puppet government. The main al Qaeda commander in Iraq, Abu Musab al-Zarqawi, has worked with Hezbollah and has operated out of Syria.

Moore accuses the United States of sacrificing morality because of greed: "The motivation for war is simple. The U.S. government started the war with Iraq in order to make it easy for U.S. corporations to do business in other countries. They intend to use cheap labor in those countries, which will make Americans rich." Yet it turns out that the self-righteous Moore's film is being heralded by a terrorist organization that has murdered and kidnapped hundreds of Americans—and also an organization that works with Zarqawi and al Qaeda. Just to avoid a boycott on a dozen screens in a totalitarian terrorist state and its colony?

Hezbollah likes the film so much that the terrorist organization has shown it on one of its television stations, according to The *New York Post*. The *Post* quotes Sheikh Hassan Nassrallah, Hezbollah's Lebanese leader, as explaining: "We may not be able to drive the Americans out of Iraq, but we can drive Bush out of the White House by heating things up in Iraq."

Theoretically, it might be possible that Moore has no personal awareness that his Middle East distributor is working with terrorists. But such ignorance is unlikely for two reasons: First, Moore's "war room" staff monitors controversial articles about the film, and there could hardly be anything more controversial than making common cause with terrorists. Not only has the Hezbollah relationship been publicized in a leading film trade on-line newspaper, the Moore-Hezbollah connection has been reported in the *Guardian*, which is one of the most significant British newspapers, and in the important American online newspaper *Salon.*

Second, Moore was personally questioned about the terrorist connection at a Washington, D.C., press conference. He at first denied the terrorist connection, but was then confronted with the direct quote from his distributor. He stonewalled and refused to answer. So the man who spends so much time getting in other people's faces with tough questions is unwilling to explain why he has not denounced the offer from Hezbollah.

The Iranian tyranny agrees with Hezbollah's appraisal of *Fahrenheit 9/11.* In mid-August 2004, according to the *New York Post,* the mullahs running the Farabi Cinema complex in Tehran scrapped the season's program to screen Moore's "documentary." Their spokesman explained, "This film unmasks the Great Satan America. It tells Muslim people why they are right in hating America."

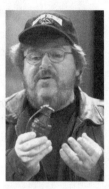

MOORE AND TERRORISM

Moore has an enormously powerful place at the pulpit—with supporters in this country and around the world. But the way he uses his pulpit is often reckless, and the ramifications can be dangerous. We know firsthand how zealous his fans in this country can be—particularly college students who feel drawn to Moore's cartoonish brand of passionate, 1960s liberalism. Without question, Moore's supporters are a fiercely devoted bunch. And that, frankly, is what worries us.

According to Moore, the United States is a violent, irrational bully. It's out to exploit the rest of the world. It's selfish and materialistic.

Newsflash: Terrorists may hate the West, but they are not isolated from its thinking. Many terrorists and almost all their leaders are quite well-educated men, often trained in Western schools. Bin Laden himself is a lawyer's son who holds a degree in engineering. 9/11 ringleader Mohamed Atta received his Master's at the University of Hamburg, where five other 9/11 hijackers were similarly educated. Zacarias Moussaoui, alleged to have been the hijacker who missed the flight, received his bachelor's degree in France, and his master's in international business in the United Kingdom. These are not Taliban in caves but people with an education. They know how to coordinate international rings, transfer millions of dollars, engineer complex bombings, or read the flight manual for a 707. Sleeper agents like the 9/11 hijackers need a good grounding in Western languages and customs, for which a European or American education is convenient. Along the way, they get a very good grounding in Western thought and popular trends. Fat'hi ash-Shiqaqi, head (until his assassination) of the Islamic Jihad, talked of enjoying Sartre; his successor, Ramadan Abdullah Shallah, was teaching politics at the University of South Florida when he received his battlefield promotion.

The ivory tower loves to play with the latest seemingly daring thoughts. Provided, of course, that they cannot be carried into reality, these offer the intellectual equivalent of a roller-coaster ride, arousing fright without any real danger. In the 1960's the dalliance was with Franz Fanon, who theorized that the Third World could only throw off the Western yoke by violence. Fanon is a difficult, plodding, read; one may doubt that any pseudo-revolutionary got past the second chapter. But they certainly read the introduction by existentialist Jean-Paul Sartre. To Sartre, colonial violence was "man recreating himself" and "rediscovering his lost innocence." For the intelligentsia, views such as these made for rich pontification, in which the rise of the West was no landmark in human cultural evolution, but rather a violent attempt to impose arbitrary and absolutist standards upon primitive, innocent, peoples.

What effect does this Western school of thought have upon Islamic radicalism? An appreciable one, actually. "Islamic fundamentalism is not an indigenous growth," John

Gray notes. "It is an exotic hybrid, bred from the encounter of sections of the Islamic intelligentsia with radical western ideologies." That's one reason why most Sunnis look on it as an "innovation"—a polite term for heresy, the belief that Islam can be fundamentally altered post-Muhammad.

Sayyid Qutb, the Egyptian founder of bin Laden's branch of radical Islam, spent time at Colorado State (and according to some accounts, Stanford University) and then toured Europe before beginning his writing. Qutbism (as his approach came to be called) draws heavily from Western thought, down to adopting Marx's concept of the stages of history with a last Islamic stage added. (In that stage, communism overcomes capitalism, and Islam then fills communism's spiritual void.)

The core religious tenet of Qutbism is that the rest of the Muslim world is becoming corrupted and drifting away from the path of true Islam. They are reverting to *Jahiliyya*, the term for Arab pagans who existed before the Koran. Qutb's years in America convinced him that the United States was a major source of the problem. Americans had decimated the Indians and oppressed the Latinos. U.S. culture centered on greed and exploitation. U.S. women were sluts and U.S. men brainless brutes. "This primitiveness can be seen in the spectacle of the fans as they follow a game of football . . . or watch boxing matches or bloody, monstrous wrestling matches. . . ." (Apart from his judgment of U.S. women, Qutb's views do seem to resemble those of a certain moviemaker at this point.) The empty materialism of the West created meaningless and unhappy lives, regardless of people's wealth.

The solution was a return to what Qutb saw as the original purity of Islam (enforced, of course, by totalitarian means). As Paul Berman, author of *Terror and Liberalism* points out, this aspect of Qutbism is quite modern, an Islamic version of Italian fascism, a drive to return to the glories of the early Caliphates rather than to those of Rome. The movement takes its religious theme from the East but its politics from the West. Qutbism is as much an ideology as a religion.

What was the major obstacle to this Koran-thumping utopia? Qutb saw the barrier, the enemy, as the West itself, in particular the United States, which would inevitably attempt to prevent the dream, driven by its needs to cloak and to protect its own moral degeneracy.

The message of Jean-Paul Sartre—through bloodshed, the revolutionary "rediscovers his lost innocence"—and his successors, adapted to the Islam, generated the underpinnings of Islamic radicalism. The West is corrupting and materialist; it inevitably infiltrates and debases the purity of the (in this case, Islamic) third world. Therein lies the origin of bin Laden's beef that the United States, by locating bases in Saudi Arabia (site of the holiest of Muslim shrines), committed a capital offense. America clearly had revealed its intentions by planting a corrupting influence in the center of Islam, in the nation which houses the holiest of Muslim shrines.

To be sure, the Middle East was not the only location where the view of America as an oppressor who must be overthrown took hold. In American and European academia, it became quite the fashion to claim that the West was *not* superior to anything else, its values were no better than any other values, and if the Third World struck back, it was no more than the West had coming. *If* by any chance some Third Worlders did have an aptitude for violence, it must be the fault of the West's past oppressions or present corruptions.

To that brew, add Michael Moore.

Moore makes the whole anti-U.S. tirade entertaining and popular. He injects these ideas into the debate:

- *Attacks on Americans are heroic and destined to succeed:* "The Iraqis who have risen up against the occupation are not "insurgents" or "terrorists" or "The Enemy." They are the REVOLUTION, the Minutemen, and their numbers will grow—and they will win."

- *And America's at fault:* "What I do know is that all day long I have heard everything about this bin Laden guy except this one fact—WE created the monster known as Osama bin Laden!"[1]

- Not only bin Laden, but anyone who wants a go at the United States is entitled to a "the devil made me do it" defense: "We have orphaned so many children, tens of thousands around the world, with our taxpayer-funded terrorism (in Chile, in Vietnam, in Gaza, in Salvador) that I suppose we shouldn't be too surprised when those orphans grow up and are a little whacked in the head from the horror we have helped cause." Or, as Moore put it only four days after 9/11: "[W]e, the United States of America, are culpable in committing so many acts of terror and bloodshed that we had better get a clue about the culture of violence in which we have been active participants."

---

[1]We might note that Moore never backs up his frequently repeated claims that bin Laden received CIA training in terror or at least combat tactics. Bin Laden's skills were in organization and finance, not in actual fighting. Moreover, in his Afghan days he was already hateful of Americans, making him an unlikely CIA contact.

- *Not to mention some conspiracy theory:* "I learned from someone at ABC News that ABC had videotape—an angle of the second plane crashing into the tower—that showed an F-16 fighter jet trailing the plane at a distance. . . . Is it becoming more clear now that the plane that went down in Pennsylvania was shot down to prevent it from attacking its destination? The truth is harrowing, unbearable—but it must be told to us." (We can add in Moore's latest theory, voiced in *Dude, Where's My Country?*—9/11 must have been committed by Saudi-trained pilots.)

- *And of course the core themes of Bowling for Columbine:* The United States is an aggressive, paranoid bully, out to destroy any Third World government that resists, a culture (if it can be called that) where materialism rules and corrupts the individual.

Sounds like Qutb wrote the screenplay, doesn't it? (Come to think of it, Qutb had a reputation as a scholar, so he would probably have done an honest job of it. It sounds more like a propagandist set out to turn Qutb's anti-American belief system into a persuasive film reflecting his views.)

Let's back up for a moment. Our point here is not that certain truths should be stifled because they are too dangerous to read. Rather, it is that a writer bears a responsibility in spreading views that are apt to incite anti-American violence, a special obligation to do his homework. Nothing excuses the irresponsible voicing of half-truths, and wild speculation, however profitable that may be.

And these views have consequences. In October 2002, two suicide bombers detonated their loads in Paddy's nightclub in

Bali, Indonesia. The blasts killed 202 people, most of them Australians and other foreign tourists. The ringleader, Imam Samudra, told police that "I saw lots of whiteys dancing and lots of whiteys drinking there," and "[t]hat place . . . was a meeting-place for U.S. terrorists and their allies." It was "Kill Whitey" (to quote a chapter heading in *Stupid White Men*) with a vengeance.

When Samudra was tried, according to the *Sydney Morning Herald,* "His lawyer, Qaidar Faisal, later delivered an official defence submission." The defense summation praised the Taliban and its version of Islam and concluded with this telling detail: "Mr. Faisal also quoted from American satirist Michael Moore's book *Stupid White Men* and other anti-western texts."

We pose a final question.

Assume, for a moment that all Moore says and writes and that what his followers absorb and then spread is accurate. The United States is an aggressive and expansionist bully, driven by material greed. It overthrows governments that get in its way and foments local wars and massacres.

Now formulate a statement about why the killing of thousands of civilians at the World Trade Center was fundamentally evil.

Not a terribly easy thing to do, is it?[2]

Postscript: It appears that Michael Moore may have a new fan. If bin Laden hasn't seen *Fahrenheit 9/11,* he's managed somehow to parallel Moore's screenplay, right down to the *My*

---

[2]If you side-step with an answer that all killing is fundamentally evil, the next assignment is to write a war crimes indictment of Franklin Delano Roosevelt and Winston Churchill.

Pet Goat story (which David Kopel, significantly, points out was not the title of the book President Bush was reading—meaning that bin Laden and Moore have somehow made the same mistake).

On November 1, 2004, just before the U.S. election, Osama bin Laden released a videotaped speech. The Arabic news outlet Al-Jazeera produced an English translation.

Bin Laden begins with what is essentially a plea of self-defense: Americans have laid waste to his nation (which nation is not specified, and it may be a mistranslation of a broader term such as "people"), and therefore "we lay waste to yours." He attributes the idea for attacking the World Trade Center to his witnessing the destruction in Lebanon in 1982.

He accuses former President George H. Bush of having become affected by (possibly the translator has in mind affection rather than affect) the wealthy monarchies in the Middle East—just as Moore stresses the ties between the Bushes and the Saudi royalty.

Then bin Laden complains of the Patriot Act and asserts it was not meant to fight terrorism: former President Bush took "dictatorship and suppression of freedoms to his son and they named it the Patriot Act, under the pretence of fighting terrorism."

He adds that the former president saw to installing his sons as state governors, who "didn't forget to import expertise in election fraud from the region's presidents to Florida." Again, this argument straight from *Fahrenheit 9/11* (if not, one wonders how bin Laden is keeping up on the Florida electoral fight from his cave).

Bin Laden then insists that the White House has waged war "to keep busy their various corporations—whether they be working in the field of arms or oil or reconstruction." Good grief, he even names Moore's favorite target, referring to "shady Bush administration-linked mega-corporations, like Halliburton and its kind."

And he trots out the *My Pet Goat* story (which did not receive much play in the general media before *Fahrenheit*, and was probably not a frequent topic of discussion among Afghan tribesmen): "It seemed to him that occupying himself by talking to the little girl about the goat and its butting was more important than occupying himself with the planes and their butting of the skyscrapers."

Bin Laden ends with what may be a reference to another Moore theme. Immediately after 9/11, Moore had written:

> Many families have been devastated tonight. This just is not right. They did not deserve to die. If someone did this to get back at Bush, then they did so by killing thousands of people who DID NOT VOTE for him! Boston, New York, DC, and the planes' destination of California—these were places that voted AGAINST Bush!

Bin Laden's message ends with a reference to the upcoming election, and to our practice of casting electoral votes by state:

> [Y]our security is not in the hands of Kerry, nor Bush, nor al-Qaida. No. Your security is in your own hands. And every State that doesn't play with our security has automatically guaranteed its own security.

The only ambiguity here is that "state" in American English can mean "one of the fifty states" or more generally, "a government." Our own Arabic is a bit rusty, but the Middle East Media Research Institute determined that bin Laden was unquestionably referring to the "fifty American States." Yigal Carmon, the president of MEMRI, explained that the Arabic term "ay wilaya" properly refers to a state or province, not a nation, and that the Islamist website Al-Qal'a had been specific: "This message was a warning to every U.S. state separately . . . it means that any U.S. state that will choose to vote for the white thug Bush as president has chosen to fight us, and we will consider it our enemy, and any state that will vote against Bush has chosen to make peace with us, and we will not characterize it as an enemy. By this characterization, Sheikh Osama wants to drive a wedge in the American body . . ."

Not targeting states that vote against Bush this time . . . the Florida 2000 election . . . the Bushes' ties to Saudi royalty . . . the Patriot Act as oppressive . . . it's not really being aimed at terror . . . waging war to benefit Haliburton . . . Bush reading the pet goat story . . . we've heard that before somewhere, haven't we?

It would certainly appear that Michael Moore has found a new fan. Or perhaps a rival, jealous of Moore's hogging the anti-American limelight in the last days before the election.

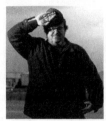

MOORE STORIES

ichael Moore has inspired a passionate grassroots movement across America, which grows stronger all the time. But it's not the one he'd hoped for.

Over the past year and a half, we've spent thousands of hours researching, writing, cataloging, and vetting other people's outstanding investigative work into Michael Moore's work and public life. Our work could never have happened were it not for the passion, dedication, and resolve of thousands of Americans united to pull back the curtain on Mike Moore.

One person e-mailed to say—before this news broke in the media—that Moore keeps a palatial mansion in Northern Michigan, which he affectionately refers to as a "cabin." Another told us how Moore's *Bowling for Columbine* was the only film released to Oscar voters on DVD, enabling them to conveniently consider it; the other four nominated films could only be seen at specially arranged screenings.

These people are the force that has filled these pages. They're the link between duplicitous documentaries created fifteen years apart. We've met, talked to, e-mailed, and interviewed hundreds just like them from all over the country—

each with a unique story to tell—for our research, our web sites, and for this book.

By far, the cruelest dismissal of these normal, everyday, average citizens is that they're somehow part of a right-wing conspiracy. The reality is that this inciting, ill-founded statement couldn't be further from the truth.

Out of all of these contributions, we have found two common themes. The first is people's distrust, anger, and disgust at Moore himself and his body of work. Nearly everybody we've come across during the course of this movement is united by a second common theme, which is often the catalyst that continues to lend this movement its reach. Chances are you, too, share a part of this common thread: Your very own *Moore Story.*

You don't have to have personally met Michael Moore to have your own Moore Story—it's far easier than that. You only need to start out, like many people do, captured by the humor and resonance of one of Moore's books or movies. Convinced that Moore speaks on your behalf—he no doubt *looks* more like most of us than the stereotype of a slick and clever Hollywood storyteller—you are, at first, naturally taken in by a man who dares to confront the larger issues that you suspect to be the root causes of your daily troubles.

Next in your own Moore Story comes revelation. Through some means—either by word of mouth or by happening on one of the many published reports out there—you discover that the Michael Moore construction you bought into is not what it appears to be. It could be a half-truth, a carefully spun statistic, or a cleverly arranged scene, edited just right to play to your emotions. But whatever it is, you learn it is a sham—and, whether instantly or over time, you come to realize that it didn't have to be this way.

It doesn't take a hard-core liberal to recognize that Moore hits on some very worthy discoveries. But it's hard to be appreciative if you're skeptical about his integrity. While a few choose to rationalize away being hoodwinked or having their ideologies sold out by Moore, most people realize that they've been temporarily taken and are simply annoyed that such a promising talent wasted his efforts on such sneaky, simplistic methods. Those that are more than annoyed—those who feel misled and betrayed on a core level—often fight back, and they have fueled the grassroots fervor.

ONE MIKE'S MOORE STORY

One Moore Story we've heard also happens to have played a large part in the creation of *Michael Moore Hates America,* a muckraking documentary currently in production. The film is attracting the attention of the masses and the media. It's a provocative rebuttal to one of Moore's biggest rants: that ordinary Americans are victimized on countless levels by an uncaring, unintelligent government and that America, as we know it, is hopeless.

Mike Wilson—the film's creator, writer, director, and chief financier—has been called the "bravest man in North America" for his bold willingness to hit Michael Moore where he lives, both in the title and content of his film in progress. He's a twenty-eight-year-old copywriter from Minneapolis whose current efforts are strikingly similar to those of Moore himself at the earliest stages of his career.

When Wilson first watched *Bowling for Columbine,* one scene in particular incensed him. Moore heads to Flint, Michigan—ground zero for many of his exploits. There, he finds the city mourning the death of six-year-old Kayla, a young girl killed by a fellow student at her elementary school. While expressing grief over the community's loss of life, Moore suggests the crime was caused in part because the killer's mother was forced to work two jobs, thanks to President Clinton's sweeping (and historic) welfare reforms. How could we expect a mother who had to work two jobs to do an adequate job raising her child? How could we expect the child to develop into a moral human being without better supervision? In other words, Moore chose to paint the mother and son as victims of a stingy, heartless political system.

This was Wilson's "Moore Story," the one that ultimately led him to embark on his counterpoint film. "The reason it hit me is that when I was growing up, my mom worked full-time, went to school full-time . . . but she was a parent," he explains. "She was a great mother. She never gave up, and it was such a slap in the face to think of my mom [while watching *Bowling*]. The message was that if you're poor but not on welfare, you're not an adequate parent. That struck me as so offensive, and started me on my journey."

WITHOUT *MOTHER JONES* MONEY

To clear the hurdle of financing the film—no *Mother Jones* settlement greasing the wheels for him—Wilson has relied primarily on two tried and true methods of guerrilla filmmaking. One is an American institution: the filmmaker's trusty credit card (see Kevin Smith's *Clerks*), subsidized heavily by an equally essential source: the kindness of strangers drawn to Wilson's fearless demonstration of an alternative voice and vision to what Moore offers. And the enthusiasm and support have not only been financial. "What's really astounding is how many people have said, 'I'm going to be first in line when this thing opens'," says Wilson. Count-less people have written him to say, "[T]he way this guy is talking about America is really contrary to how we feel and what we think about the country."

To get their message out, though, first they'll have to fin-ish filming. The original goal was to raise the more than $400,000 needed to effectively produce and market the movie to the widest audience (through a distribution com-pany). Though they may fall short of that mark, there's no thought of giving up. With hopes of a release date around the same time Moore's *Fahrenheit 9/11* hits theaters in summer 2004, Wilson and his crew still have many interviews, writ-ing, editing, and publicity left to do.

Not to mention, they're still looking for Michael Moore.

THE BIG AMERICAN CONVERSATION

Even if Wilson can't track down Moore for the "official" inter-view he's seeking, he's already found him once, and it's given him great footage to illustrate the first of his points: that the shrillness of Moore's arguments creates a false sense of doom and negativity around our nation.

October 11, 2003: Michael Moore is traveling the country to promote *Dude, Where's My Country?*, with his next stop set for what Mike Wilson calls "one of the most liberal colleges in America," the University of Minnesota. There, Moore gives a speech that generates loud cheers from his audience of col-lege students, allowing for a brief series of questions near the end. It is then that Wilson has his chance at the microphone, echoing the famous scene in *Roger & Me* where a young Michael Moore confronts GM's chairman Roger Smith at a 1988 shareholder's meeting.

The crowd of several thousand Moore supporters falls temporarily silent. "I'm making a documentary called *Michael Moore Hates America,*" Wilson tells Moore. "It's more innocuous than it sounds, and I'm really just interested in the big American conversation."

With that, Wilson had given Moore all the information he needed to explode into one of his much publicized rants. With his crowd fully behind him, "whipped into a frenzy," as Wilson described them, Moore didn't shut down Wilson's microphone. Instead, Moore castigated Wilson, tossing in a legal threat for good measure. As Wilson describes it, "He shouted, 'Everything I do is because I love America! It's people like you who hate America! You hate America! What you just said was slander!'"

After the event, Wilson spoke to Moore supporters outside the auditorium, where he noted a marked change in the tone. Outside, there was no frenzied screaming, only friendly and intelligent dialogue. "All in all," wrote Wilson after the event, "I have to say that those conversations afterward were so rewarding and moving. It's empowering to know that people can still have a one-on-one conversation without resorting to shrillness . . . unless, of course, you're Michael Moore."

SO WHAT ABOUT THE REST OF THE COUNTRY?

To illustrate his next argument, Wilson again echoes the early technique of Michael Moore, turning the camera toward himself. Here, the film delves into the personal, revealing the antithesis of Moore's portrayal of the welfare victim in *Bowling*. Wilson interviews his own father, who had recently been laid off but was refreshingly optimistic about it.

This introduces Wilson's most meaningful cause in the movie: Optimism, with a capital O.

In another similarity with Moore's *Roger & Me,* Wilson also adds his own story to the mixture, describing how he also lost his job during the midst of filming. This unlucky turn gave Wilson more fuel, however, as it allowed him to devote more time to working on the movie. He began to test his own theory about overcoming hardship by rolling up one's sleeves.

With more free time and a renewed resolve, Wilson then set out across the country to see if the inspiration his parents provided held true in the streets of the country.

He barbecued on a street called Columbine in California and played hockey in the closed-off strip of road in front of the White House. Everywhere he's gone, Wilson has been continually impressed with the evidence he's seen that the country is not, as Moore would have us believe, a wasteland of desperation and entitlement. "As I played goalie for a few minutes in front of the home of the most powerful man in the world," Wilson wrote in a letter to supporters, "I really began to grasp how amazing our American way of life is. *And we filmed it all.* It's not like you see the French playing sports in front of Chirac's place."

Wilson's quest to document an alternative reality—an antithesis to the despair that Moore fills his movies with—has also led him to question not just regular people but more notable ones as well. So far, he's talked to David Horowitz, a former liberal activist who's now squarely for the other side; as well as Senator Norm Coleman and former college football star and congressman J. C. Watts. Other big names are in the works as well.

Perhaps the most notable name to appear so far is Penn Jillette, the often misunderstood magician, comedian, pitchman, TV star (Showtime's *Bullshit*), and talkative half of Penn & Teller. Jillette's interview introduces *Michael Moore Hates America*'s third theme, and it's a notion that Michael Moore himself would likely embrace: that all documentaries are altered versions of reality and that the process of first filming and then editing true events makes them inherently untrue—or at least markedly less true.

It sounds simple, but to hear Penn tell it will reshape the way you think about everything from local TV news to even the seemingly objective congressional coverage on C-SPAN. And to prove Penn's theories and show once and for all how Moore is able to distort reality to fit his aims, Wilson and his producer have devised a unique experiment.

With permission of the NRA, they've collected the exact same footage used by Michael Moore during the filming of the Columbine/NRA Meeting scenes in *Bowling*. Wilson will then recut the footage, this time designed to present the events closer to how they actually occurred. The intention is not what you may think—not to prove that Heston is innocent, but rather that Heston is neither—he is simply a pawn, a device, used by Moore that can easily be shaped to advance any idea.

And if a few short scenes can be molded into nearly anything, what does that say about nearly everything else that Moore has filmed? Wilson warns against taking the grey area of the documentary as hard and fast fact—we all, as viewers, must learn to weigh what we're told and not merely accept it blindly.

The irony of his film is not lost on Mike Wilson. He is David to the Goliath that Michael Moore has become. No longer the ambitious, idealistic activist of his youth, Moore has transformed into that which he purports to hate the most: a very rich, pasty-white, manipulative behemoth. And so it has come full circle, as a young filmmaker—eager to expose fraud and empower people with his message—follows hot on Moore's heels, challenging him as fully and as critically as Moore himself challenged GM with 1989's *Roger & Me.*

Although he has not yet interviewed Moore, other than their brief encounter at the University of Minnesota, Mike Wilson has indeed found him. By exposing Moore's methods as fallacies passing for facts, and proving, despite what Moore needs us to believe, that America is still full of intelligent, hard-working people who care about things beyond their own self-interest, Wilson is offering an alternative vision of American possibility—and filling a gap that sorely needed to be filled.

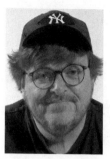

CLOSING THOUGHTS

I f all of his character assassinations were tried as criminal offenses, Michael Moore would stand out as the greatest repeat offender in modern history. His path to this distinction is a remarkable one.

In *Roger & Me* Moore discovered that he could play with the truth, and audiences and critics would accept it so long as he entertained them. The film's wicked humor derives from the portrayal of Flint's moronic attempts to offset the economic depression. In fact, Moore had cooked up the cause-and-effect equation on which the film hinges. The city's initiatives had been undertaken years before the worst unemployment occurred. But Moore *did* entertain and turning $58,000 into several million was a reasonable return. Particularly since a large majority of his viewers never did learn that he'd played with the facts, and many of this percentage became ardent fans and supporters of his work.

When Moore was cornered on his departure from the truth, he quickly sprang back with what we recognize now as his two routine dodges. First, he refused to characterize *Roger & Me* as a documentary, as if that relieved him from an obligation to be totally accurate. When Harlan Jacobson, the first critic to blow the whistle on the credibility of *Roger & Me*, asked Moore if he considered the film to be a documentary, Moore said that he intended the film to be "an entertaining movie, like *Sophie's Choice*." Second, Moore ignored questions about his suspect methodology, and jumped straight into an conspiracy theory spun around his critics. It would become a trend: Anyone who raised objections to Moore's works became instantly transformed, in his eyes, into a puppet for the many mysterious forces arrayed against him. Why, Harlan Jacobson wrote for *Film Comment, Film Comment* was funded by Lincoln Center, and Lincoln Center had received a grant from General Motors (GM). In Moore's world, this convoluted network was adequate grounds to dismiss the real points that Jacobson had forced him to admit during the interview.

At least one could say that if the falsified portions of *Roger & Me* were deleted, there would still be a documentary left. GM *had* laid off thousands in the name of raising profits by moving to Mexico, it *had* shown little if any loyalty to its workforce or its community, and the lot of those left unemployed *was* often heartbreaking. That aspect, the existence of some core truth, would steadily fade from Moore's focus as he continued on his career trajectory. He had found that wealth and fame could be achieved by clever and misleading editing presented as fact, and that the only real consequence was a hefty bank account.

By the time he published *Stupid White Men*, Moore had crossed an important line: He'd started to take himself seriously and had become one more ranting pontificator among many on our political scene. Still, this new self-seriousness conveniently gave way when CNN's Lou Dobbs asked him about *Stupid White Men*'s alleged inaccuracies, and Moore famously replied "How can there be inaccuracy in comedy?"

His departures from the truth became more frequent and more blatant. One wonders how he could write that 200,000 Americans have mad cow disease, that the Pentagon spent five-sixths of its budget on a single model of an airplane, or that 31 percent of black Florida males eligible to vote have a felony conviction. Did he wonder whether anyone was going to believe it? Well, whether or not people believed it, they certainly bought it—as evidenced by the length of time the book stayed on best-seller lists both in the United States and in Germany. The lesson that tossing around misrepresentations as factual information is not only acceptable but massively profitable was reinforced.

And there was another important lesson: In *Roger & Me*, Moore had learned that people will pay to see other people ridiculed, and yuppies will pay handily for the privilege of laughing at and feeling superior to working people.

And, as one might expect from the title, in *Stupid White Men* Moore plays this theme to the max. The real intention of his attack on George W. Bush's Cabinet is to make the reader feel superior to all of them; our leaders are the real collection of losers. Is America a "nation of idiots"? Well, at least the reader has millions of other Americans to look down on (never mind that we're actually doing well by world literacy standards, the important thing is to be able to look down your nose at others). Moore's followers can feel smugly superior to about 80 percent of the country using his own figures on the national moron population.

With *Stupid White Men*, Moore again raked in millions and discovered that he had a market overseas. Europeans would pay very well for the privilege of feeling superior to the upstart Americans who had gone, in the lapse of a century, from being a Third World country (a fair description of us in 1850, with a small swampy town for a capital, human slavery, no transcontinental railroad, and a 5,000 man military) to a superpower—and in half a century more, to being the *only* superpower.

The result of these lessons learned was *Bowling for Columbine,* a documentary in which the viewer is fed vague theories and misled by half-truths. The viewer is shown supposed presidential campaign ads that were actually manipulated in Moore's editing shop by joining the real Bush campaign ad from a different campaign with invented captions added. The viewer hears people giving speeches that they never gave, their words edited into new configurations intended to inspire the audience's hatred. Moore has no compunction in painting a leader of the civil rights movement as a racist, in claiming that the NRA—an organization founded by Union officers and chartered by New York's legislature—is a parallel group to the Ku Klux Klan. His editing techniques, still a bit rough in *Roger,* have now fully evolved. He can take a speech and turn it into whatever he desires, skillfully using images and other footage to hide the cuts. One cannot fairly compare Moore to the Stalinist propagandists: Next to him, they were oafs with a cheap tape recorder.

Moore is by now taking himself *very* seriously. Self-assured in his defeat of GM, he is out to smite larger enemies—Republicans, defense contractors, Charlton Heston, the NRA, perhaps even the United States itself—and truth has never been more expendable in his crusade.

Roger & Me at least had some remaining value after the misleading parts were deducted. But remove those from *Bowling* and naught remains. The United States has a high rate of firearms violence. This much is true. Then a fellow named Moore goes searching for the reasons and comes up empty. Undeterred, he attributes the stats to welfare reform, bombing in Kosovo, increasing gun ownership, rising media coverage of crime—all of which actually coincide with a record *decline* in homicide rates. What a documentary Bowling could've been, had it actually spent more time talking with those close to the Columbine tragedy and less time chasing Dick Clark for comedic effect.

That Moore created a piece of fiction, spiced up by personal antagonism and character assassination, did not stop him from picking up an Oscar and several more millions. Indeed, groups struggled to invent new awards for his brilliance. For the first time in decades, the Cannes Film Festival recognized a documentary and Moore qualified for a prize. The Screenwriters Guild handed him the award for best screenplay—despite the fact that documentaries don't have traditional screenplays. (A screenplay is a script, with description of actors' characters, and the dialogue they must deliver. Apart from re-creations, documentaries don't have actors or characters, and the dialogue is created by the people interviewed, not by Moore.) Again, the lesson was reinforced: Fiddle with the truth, and people will fall all over themselves rushing to bestow awards and wealth on you. And the considerable scrutiny that has befallen *Bowling* has not dismayed Cannes organizers. This year, they gave Moore first prize, assuring his *Fahrenheit 9/11* of an audience to help launch its box office hopes.

From *Bowling* it was a modest step to Moore's most inaccurately comedic masterwork, *Dude, Where's My Country?* Moore continued to edit facts to create his own truth, but now a new element crept in: Paranoia. A certain degree of paranoia goes hand in hand with narcissism: The narcissist's discovery of plots invisible to the ordinary person demonstrates his superior insight, and his discovery of plots directed at himself proves that, yes, the world really does revolve around him. At a certain level, *Dude* is a liberal black helicopter tale. Why, Moore moans, his previous publisher dared to delay his book, merely because it was due out the day after 9/11, attacked the United States and its President, and had a chapter titled "Kill Whitey"! How dare they allow national tragedy to interfere with his expectations and demands!

Moore goes on in *Dude* to present conspiracy after conspiracy, each with either no evidence or with a handful of facts blurred together and slanted heavily to achieve the desired impression. Bin Laden is tied to Bush. Never mind that the statement is based on the fact that relatives of bin Laden (who have disowned him) keep money with the same international investment firm as relatives of George W. Bush. What's more, Moore insists, Bin Laden didn't do it—it must have been pilots from the Saudi Air Force, because only they could have hit the mark. Mysterious government planes flew around picking up bin Ladens, while the rest of us were grounded, and got them out of the country before the FBI could question them. No need to clarify that the planes weren't government-owned, it didn't happen while all planes were grounded, the bin Ladens at last report remained in the United States for over a week, and the FBI approved. The war in Afghanistan wasn't launched in response to the terror attacks, but undertaken to clear a path for an oil pipeline backed by President Bush. Unsurprisingly, Moore fails to note that Bush *wasn't* backing that pipeline or that a fellow named Bill Clinton *was*.

CLOSING THOUGHTS

And then came *Fahrenheit 9/11*. The highest grossing documentary feature of all time. It was conceived, promoted, and has now become Moore's masterpiece, his labor of true love (and hate).

Moore's hope with *Fahrenheit 9/11* was that the voters across the entire country would take their cue from him, believing whatever conspiracies he unveiled in the key months prior to the election. Indeed, it was meant as (and became) a watershed event in American politics: the longest, most expensive, and most legally questionable campaign commercial ever produced specifically to unseat an incumbent president.

Though he failed—spectacularly, in fact—Moore's intentions were nonetheless as grandiose as they come, such that he is completely unique in world history: Via *Fahrenheit 9/11*, he hoped not to be crowned king of the United States, but better, its kingmaker.

The next head on Moore's platter is likely to be that of America's health care industry. He hopes to release a documentary—tentatively titled *Sicko*—in late 2005 or early 2006.

While little is known about its contents, like his earlier work, Moore's most predictable themes—supported by his equally-tiresome means of *proving* his "truths"—are both likely to surface in *Sicko*.

There's a catch though: In producing the film, no longer can Moore apply his methods of trickery and coercion in secret, only to wade through the inevitable minor backlashes after the film's impact has already been widespread. In fact, wary forewarnings of his methods are already appearing in health care company newsletters and have—unlike the past—been picked up by the mainstream media quite a while *before* the film reaches audiences.

Before it even fades in, the film will likely begin with a ruthless disregard for the truth. The narcissist, as Dr. Vaknin wrote, is a pathological liar by nature, a man who either believes his own fabrications or regards lying as morally neutral.

This time around, however, reports have already surfaced about health care companies warning employees not to talk to Moore. The warnings may force him to adopt new tactics, but they haven't deterred him: at least five major health care companies have already reported Moore sightings at their offices nationwide. One company even suggested Moore had hired actors to pose as corrupt pharmaceutical employees in an unsurprisingly dishonest attempt to expose a few doctors as quacks (and by extension, indict the entire profession).

Of course, the most salacious of these rumors cannot be confirmed. Did anybody really expect Moore to become that sloppy when millions in box office—and now, his credibility—are at stake?

If he *is* able to rebound from the public embarrassment suffered in his failed bid to bring down a president, the debut of *Sicko* could prove to be a fitting capstone to quite a self-serving career. The pity, as always, is that Moore's work is built on so many savaged victims, people held up for ridicule or public detestation who did nothing to deserve either: Larry Stecco, Charlton Heston, Al Gore, Joe Leiberman, and George W. Bush alike. In fact, we're all victims of Moore's rambling attacks. With these assaults, designed to viciously tear down the target, Moore is promoting a society-wide drift toward the very self-focus, mean-spiritedness, selfishness, malignant cynicism and lack of ethics that have characterized his career.

CLOSING THOUGHTS

The message being conveyed is that the United States is hopelessly corrupt, violent, aggressive, and thrives by invading and destroying the spiritually, politically, and environmentally pristine regions of the world. Further, the United States is inhabited and led by morons, lunatics, and a government that, according to Moore, teeters on the edge of morphing into Nazi Germany.

Fahrenheit 9/11 gave Moore a global platform. A case can be made that Moore's theories give terrorists a reasonable defense for their attempts at murdering the American way of life. Moore suggests that almost all world violence has an American cause, which suggests that striking America is morally justified. In many ways, Moore's message echoes that of the Moslem extremist Qutb—but Moore, of course, has a multimedia pulpit and an enormous audience. Any follower of Qutbism—a category that includes bin Laden and his boys—will find Moore's work proof of their worst fears, with the confirmation coming straight from inside America itself.

There is an issue of social responsibility to be considered here. Moore's core message, based largely on falsehoods constructed for emotional effect, is that America is corrupt and invasive of the rest of the globe. The net effect of that message is to create a political and social atmosphere in which terrorism is not seen as the immoral and inherently evil pursuit that it is.

Moore's bending the truth to promote and popularize this atmosphere of Anti-Americanism may not be the direct cause of any crimes that follow. But it is certainly legitimate to question whether Moore's reckless grandstanding and ill-founded polemics, while profitable for himself, does his countrymen more harm than good.

Bill Bailey, a good friend, once suggested that in our country the proper remedy for abuse of freedom of speech is even more freedom of speech. This book reflects our effort to apply that remedy to Michael Moore. The important thing is that the dialogue has begun, one that invites you as the reader to judge the truth of these matters for yourself.

In the end, that is what our country—the one that has bestowed upon Michael Moore all its many riches—is most firmly about.

NOTES AND SOURCES

MICHAEL MOORE'S RÉSUMÉ

Moore began *Mother Jones* tenure by telling staff he would not have printed one article that they had printed in the last three issues: Available from www.faqs.org/faqs/celebrities/michael-moore-faq/part1.

Moore says he was too much of a journalist for *Mother Jones*, but *Mother Jones* says he was impossible to work with: Rick Marin, "The Truth about Michael Moore," *Washington Times* (February 14, 1990), and available from www.salon.com/june97/media/media970606.html. See also www.movies.yahoo.com/shop?d=hc&id=1800064216&cf=biog&intl=us.

Moore founds "Moore's Weekly" while working for Nader: Ibid.

Moore's statement that Nader hired him when he was broke and unemployed and his reference to Nader's pettiness and eccentricity: Available from Moore's web site: www.michaelmoore.com/words/message/index.php?messageDate=2001-05-04.

Moore's claim that Nader asked him to leave because Nader was jealous of his book advance and the response that he was not showing up for work: Larissa Macfarquhar, "The Populist," *New Yorker* (February 16, 2004), p. 133. Available from www.newyorker.com/printable/?fact/040216fa_fact7.

NOTES AND SOURCES

Moore's alienation of the *TV Nation* employees: Ibid.

The NBC decision to kill *TV Nation:* Available from www.faqs. org/faqs/celebrities/michael-moore-faq/part1. The Fox decision to do the same is documented at www.faqs.org/faqs/celebrities/ michael-moore-faq/part1 and www.movies.yahoo.com/shop?d=hc&id= 1800064216&cf=biog&intl=us.

That the Writer's Guild had to be called into arbitrate disputes with Moore: Michael Moore, "Michael Moore Fires Back," *Salon* (July 3, 1997). Available from www.salon.com/july97/ moore970703.html.

Disputes between Moore and studio held up release of *Canadian Bacon* for two years: Available from www.faqs.org/faqs/celebrities/ michael-moore-faq/part3.

Canadian Bacon's box office standing: *TV Guide* gave *Canadian Bacon* two stars and rated it as "puerile, thinly veiled remake" of *Dr. Strangelove.* Canadian critic Ryan Cracknell considered it an "unfunny and unenlightening satire." Available from www.rottentomatoes. com/click/movie-1063811/reviews.php?critic=columns&sortby= default&page=1&rid=1188127. It received a half-star rating from all-reviews.com www.all-reviews.com/videos-4/canadian-bacon.htm.

Moore's dispute with Borders bookstore: Available from www. labournet.net/ukunion/9912/borders4.html.

Moore's claim that Borders is using *Salon* to libel him: Available from www.interesting-people.org/archives/interesting-people/199611/ msg00091.html and discussed in Daniel Radosh, "Michael Moore Fires Back," *Salon* (July 3, 1997). Available from www.salon. com/july97/moore970703.html.

Moore's experience at the 2001 Writer's Guild award dinner: Available from his web page at www.michaelmoore.com/words/message/ index.php?messageDate=2001-03-07.

Moore's battle with HarperCollins is discussed in numerous sources (Moore mentioned it repeatedly during the time following publication.) A typical reference: Available from www.alternet.org/ story.html?StoryID=12577. The same article discusses his claims that HarperCollins was sabotaging his distribution.

Moore's comment that in the wake of his Oscar booing *Bowling's* theater attendance doubled and *Stupid White Men* again became a bestseller: Available from his web page at www.michaelmoore.com/words/message/index.php?messageDate=2003-04-08.

A few of the many articles generated by Moore's claims that Disney had refused to distribute *Fahrenheit 9/11:* Christy Lemire, "Michael Moore's Sept. 11 Documentary Looking for Distributor," *San Diego Union-Tribune* (May 5, 2004). Available from www.signonsandiego.com/news/nation/20040505-1355-disney-michaelmoore.html; "Disney Blocks New Michael Moore Doco," Australian Broadcasting Corp. (May 5, 2004). Available from www.abc.net.au/lateline/content/2004/s1103134.htm. The *New York Times* editorial nominating Disney for a gold medal for cowardice is "Disney's Craven Behavior," *New York Times* (May 6, 2004). Available from www.nytimes.com/2004/05/06/opinion/06THU4.html?ex=1084420800&en=dd695e1433b69ff3&ei=5062&partner=GOOGLE.

Moore's admission that he had known for nearly a year that Disney would not be the American distributor: Discussed in Andrew Gumbel, "Moore Admits Disney 'Ban' Was a Stunt," *Independent* [UK] (May 7, 2004). Available from www.news.independent.co.uk/world/americas/story.jsp?story=518901.

AN OPEN LETTER TO MICHAEL MOORE

"Wacko attackos" is a term coined by Moore on his web site answering critics of *Bowling for Columbine:* Available from www.michaelmoore.com/words/wackoattacko.

Moore's claims about Polygram burying *Canadian Bacon:* "The Movies & Me," Michael Moore, *The Nation,* November 4, 1996, p. 10.

Moore responds to *Salon* criticism with a statement that it is sponsored by Borders books, which stopped him from speaking: "Michael Moore Fires Back at *Salon*," *Salon* (July 3, 1997). Available from www.salon.com/july97/moore970703.html. Moore claims that the President is sending "his henchmen" after him is found on his "Wacko Attacko" page at www.michaelmoore.com/words/wackoattacko.

THE PROPHET OF THE LEFT IS NEVER RIGHT

GM's annual profits rising by $1.5 billion: Available from www.multinationalmonitor.org/hyper/issues/1990/01/mm0190_12 .html; (1989 profits $4.22 billion) and www.multinationalmonitor. org/hyper/issues/1990/01/mm0190_03.html; (1995 GM profits $5.9 billion). See also www.wsws.org/public_html/prioriss/iwb2-12/ gm.htm.

Moore's prediction that bombing will never bring down Milosevic: Available from www.commondreams.org/kosovo/views/mmoore.htm. Milosevic's subsequent downfall is chronicled at www.newsaic.com/ casemilosevic.html.

Moore's statement that Nader's campaign led to the Democrats gaining control of the Senate: Michael Moore, *Stupid White Men* (New York: HarperCollins, 2002), p. 239. His criticism of Cheney for reluctance to sell Haliburton Stock is from the same text, p. 17.

Moore's statement opposing the Afghan war: Available from www.michaelmoore.com/words/message/index.php?messageDate= 2001-09-14.

Mel Gibson's refusal to finance *Fahrenheit 9/11:* Available from www.worldnetdaily.com/news/article.asp?ARTICLE_ID=32518.

Miramax's decision to fund the *Fahrenheit 9/11:* Available from www.americandaily.com/item/2702.

The removal of Michael Eisner as Disney's CEO, in light of stock price slumps: *Fahrenheit 9/11:* Available from www.adage.com/ news.cms?newsId=39963.

Moore's endorsement of the Dixie Chicks and proclamation of their rising popularity: Available from www.globalaware.org/noticeboard/ mm_dixie.html.

The Dixie Chicks' announcement that they are withdrawing from country music: Available from www.gopusa.com/news/2003/ september/0926_dixie_chicks.shtml.

Moore endorsed Wesley Clark and predicted that he would beat Bush: Available from Mike's Messages at www.michaelmoore.com/words/message/index.php?messageDate=2004-01-14.

Moore's statement that the Dean revolution must not end is taken from the same source: Available from www.michaelmoore.com/words/message/index.php?messageDate=2004-01-20.

The announcement that French President Chirac will meet with President Bush: Available from www.cnn.netscape.cnn.com/ns/news/story.jsp?id=200403241451000029262598&dt=20040324145100&w=RTR&coview=.

FIRST OFFENSE: *ROGER & ME*

Moore's introduction to Hamper's book: Available from www.michaelmoore.com/hamper/chapter1.html.

Moore's speaker's bureau description of himself as born in Flint: Available from www.greatertalent.com/bios/moore.shtml.

Moore's web page claiming that he is a Flint native: Available from www.michaelmoore.com/books-films/index.php.

Moore's production company web page describing him as born in Flint: Available from www.dogeatdogfilms.com/books/mmbio.html.

Moore's empathy is a function of growing up in Flint: Ron Sheldon, "Exclusive Interview with Michael Moore of TV Nation," *People's Weekly World* (September 23, 1995). Available from www.pww.org/archives95/95-09-23-3.html.

Moore biographies stating he was born in Flint, hometown of Flint, and so on: Available from www.readersroom.com/cjmay04.html, www.michaelmoore.com/books-films/index.php, and www.michaelmoore.com/books-films/index.php.

Moore's birth in Davison: Available from www.faqs.org/faqs/celebrities/michael-moore-faq/part1/.

There is some question about whether Moore resided in Flint at all. I spoke to one of Moore's high school classmates. Moore went to school in Davison, Michigan—25 miles east of Flint. "Growing up in Davison and telling the world you are from Flint is like growing up in Bloomfield Hills and saying you are from Detroit," Moore's classmate said. "It just doesn't cut it."

Moore confirms his Davison upbringing: Michael Moore, "Weather Report," *Flint Voice* (June 3–16, 1982), p. 2 (referring to "my senior year at Davison High School" and "those of us who lived in Davison").

Demographic information on Flint, Burton, and Davison: Available from www.encyclopedia.thefreedictionary.com/Davison,%20Michigan, www.city-data.com/city/Davison-Michigan.html, www.city-data.com/city/Flint-Michigan.html and www.city-data.com/city/Burton-Michigan.html. In 2000, the median household income and median house value were: Flint: $28,015/$49,700; Davison $37,482/$100,000; Burton $44,500/$84,500. Davison's poverty rate was 6.7 percent, compared to a national average of 11.3 percent. Available from www.census.gov/Press-Release/www/2001/cb01-158.html.

Moore's production firm web page describing the *Flint Voice* and *Michigan Voice:* Available from www.dogeatdogfilms.com/books/mmbio.html.

University flyers describing, in identical words, the Michigan voice as one of the nation's most respected alternative newspapers: Available from Columbia University: www.jrn.columbia.edu/events/reuters/2001-03-21.asp; University of Wisconsin: www.uwec.edu/NewsBureau/bulletin/past/1997-98/11-24-97/bulletin.html; College of Wooster; www.wooster.edu/news/0304/ForumMoore.php.

Financial data on the *Michigan Voice: Michigan Voice* (July/August 1984), p. 2. The same issue points out that the newspaper's monthly income was $3,200, its expenditures $8,070, and the difference was largely being met by "generous contributions from Herman Warsh, Stewart Mott, and Sandy Chapin."

Moore's intro to Hamper's *Rivethead:* Available from www.michaelmoore.com/hamper/chapter1.html.

Moore's claims that *Mother Jones* management complained of Hamper's writing: Available from www.findarticles.com/cf_0/m1548/n6_v13/21248742/p3/article.jhtml?term=.

Hamper's letter from *Mother Jones'* managing editor: Larissa Macfarquhar, "The Populist," *New Yorker* (February 16, 2004), p. 133.

Moore's claim that Nader asked him to leave: Macfarquhar, "The Populist."

Moore's editorial noting Flint's 26 percent unemployment rate: Michael Moore, "Weather Report," *Michigan Voice* (September 1984), p. 10.

The origins of *Roger & Me* in Mike Westfall's ideas were established by the authors' personal communications with Mr. Westfall, who provided written evidence and supporting statements of other activists who had known Moore while he was preparing the film. The appropriation of the idea is also documented in Ed Bradley, "Moore Response to Nader: Sour Grapes," *Flint Journal* (January 20, 1990), p. C-1, and in Rick Marin, "The Truth About Michael Moore," *Washington Times* (February 14, 1990), p. E-1. See also Ed Bradley, "Moore Mistaken?" *Flint Journal* (January 31, 1990), p. E-1, and Chris Thompson, "Roger & Me Dwells on Sore Points While Healing Is Needed," *Saginaw News* (February 3, 1990).

Moore's response to Phil Donahue is from a transcript of the January 29, 1990, *Phil Donahue Show.*

Nader's denial that his office had sent a letter disavowing Mike Westfall and the others and Moore's claim that Nader's people were trying to extort money from him is from Ed Bradley, op. cit. (January 20, 1990).

Article claiming Moore was "notoriously snubbed" for the Oscar in 1990: Available from www.docurama.com/Docurama/docnewsarticledetail.html?newsid=37&bid=1653.

The Harlan Jacobson interview: Harlan Jacobson, "Michael & Me." *Film Comment* (November/December 1989), beginning on p. 16.

One in four families were GM workers: Rick Marin, "The Truth About Michael Moore and *Roger & Me,*" *Washington Times* (February 14, 1990).

NOTES AND SOURCES

Further discrepancies in the film: Elaine Dutka, "Will Controversy Cost 'Roger' an Oscar?" *Los Angeles Times* (January 17, 1990) p. 1.

Moore's quote assailing Lincoln Center and GM: Available from www.faqs.org/faqs/celebrities/michael-moore-faq/part1.

Harlan Jacobson's statement that he with drew from film criticism because of "backlash from a dispute with filmmaker Michael Moore about the accuracy of Moore's film Roger and Me": Steve Manning, "Alumni Profiles." Available from www.haverford.edu/publications/fall97/jacobson.html.

Roger Smith never stayed at the Waldorf Astoria nor belonged to Grosse Pointe Yacht Club: Patrick Lee, "Exasperated GM Chief Pans Satiric Film as 'Sick Humor'," *Los Angeles Times* (January 4, 1990), p. 6.

Moore's response to Pauline Kael's criticism: Available from www.michaelmoore.com/words/message/index.php?messageDate=2000-01-12.

Moore claim that the Oscar documentary committee wants to punish films that reach a broader audience: Jack Newfield, "An Interview with Michael Moore." Available from www.tikkun.org/magazine/index.cfm/action/tikkun/issue/tik9811/article/981114c.html.

Information about the lawsuit filed by Larry Stecco: Taken from personal conversations with his attorney, Glen Lenhoff (April, 2004).

The Court of Appeals ruling reversing the $4.5 million award against Moore's production firm: *Scalamandre v. Kaufman*, 113 F.3d 556 (5th Cir. 1997). The case keys on American constitutional restrictions which (as applied by the Supreme Court) impose a heavy burden on any "public figure" that sues for defamation. In "public figure" cases the person suing must prove, by "clear and convincing evidence," not merely that he was falsely defamed but that the speaker or writer acted with "actual malice" (meaning something very close to "had actual knowledge it was false"). It appears from the opinion that Moore himself (not yet wealthy) was either not sued, or was one of the defendants dropped just prior to trial. As a result, plaintiffs would have had to prove actual malice against the production firm, which probably had no idea that the program was false.

The Pauline Kael quotes: Pauline Kael, review of *Roger & Me*, "Roger & Me," *New Yorker* (January 8, 1990) pp. 90–93.

STUPID WHITE MEN: THE GOSPEL ACCORDING TO MICHAEL

Brady Act requirements of record destruction: 18 U.S. Code § 922(t)(2)(C).

Moore claims that Gale Norton wrote opinions against the National Environmental Protection Act and declared the Endangered Species Act unconstitutional: Michael Moore, *Stupid White Men* (New York: HarperCollins, 2002) p. 21.

Moore's criticism of Colin Powell and Condoleezza Rice: Moore, *Stupid White Men*, p. 22.

"Nation of idiots": Ibid. p. 85.

Moore's statement that 45 million Americans are functionally illiterate: Moore, *Stupid White Men*, p. 86, and the end-note attributing this to the National Center for Educational Statistics is on p. 264. The same study revealed at19 percent of those surveyed had visual difficulties, many were recent immigrant who might still be learning English, and thousands were in prison: see National Center for Educational Statistics, *Executive Summary of Adult Literacy in America: A First Look at the Results of the National Adult Literacy Survey*. Available from www.nces.ed.gov/naal/resources/execsumm. asp and www.nces.ed.gov/naal/resources/execsumm.asp.

Moore's claim that the United States goes out of its way to remain ignorant: Moore, *Stupid White Men*, p. 87.

The UNESCO international survey of literacy is discussed in the National Institute for Literacy, International Adult Literacy Survey Overview, available online at www.nifl.gov/nifl/facts/IALS.html.

An example of Moore's use of the "dumbest Brit is smarter than smartest American" gimmick: Martin Kettle, "Michael Moore,"

Guardian (November 13, 2002), p. 000. Available from www. guardian.co.uk/arts/reviews/story/0,11712,839025,00.html.

The National Geographic announcement of the 2002 survey results: Bijal P. Trivedi, "Survey Reveals Geographic Illiteracy," *National Geographic*, November 20, 2002. Online at www.news.nationalgeographic. com/news/2002/11/1120_021120_GeoRoperSurvey.html. The survey itself can be found at www.nationalgeographic.com/geosurvey/ download/RoperSurvey.pdf.

The report of the Canadian Broadcasting Company fouling up the map of North America: "The Art of Map-Making," *Ottawa Citizen* (November 19, 2003). Available from www.fpinfomart.ca/ar/ar_ result.php?page=1.

The errors on the map at Ottawa's airport: Janice Kennedy, "Take That, Atlanta: Exacting Our Geographical Revenge," *Ottawa Citizen* (October 25, 2003). Available from www.canada.com/ottawa/ ottawacitizen/specials/styleweekly/story.html?id=A578C8A3-1298- 4509-8F43-17DFA80918DC.

Moore claims that hundreds of thousands of Americans suffer from Mad Cow Disease: Moore, *Stupid White Men*, p. 137.

Deborah Rogers' article on which Moore's claim is based and which he grossly misinterprets: Deborah S. Rogers, "Mad Cow Here? It's the Wrong Question," *Star Tribune* [Minneapolis, MN] (April 2, 2001).

Moore's advice on prions and cooking meat: Moore, *Stupid White Men*, p. 137.

On George W. Bush's supposed $190 million campaign fund given by big donors: Moore's own source says $190 million was "soft money": Don Van Natta Jr. and John M. Broder, "The Few, the Rich, the Rewarded Donate the Bulk of G.O.P. Gifts," *New York Times* (August 2, 2000). Available from www.commondreams.org/ headlines/080200-03.htm.

On Democratic Party's raising of soft money from big donors: Ruth Marcus and Dan Balz, "Democrats Have Fresh Doubts on 'Soft

Money' Ban," *Washington Post* (March 5, 2001). Available from www.commondreams.org/headlines01/0305-01.htm.

Documentation of Hillary Clinton soft money: "OpenSecrets," *Money in Politics Alert,* vol. 5, no. 58 (September 29, 2000). Available from www.opensecrets.org/alerts/v5/alertv5_58.asp.

Major donor was responsible for getting Monica Lewinsky her internship: "OpenSecrets," *Money in Politics Alert,* vol. 5, no. 58 (September 29, 2000). Available from www.opensecrets.org/alerts/v5/alertv5_58.asp.

Moore's assertion that Fred Barnes had no knowledge of the *Iliad* and *Odyssey:* Moore, *Stupid White Men,* pp. 91–92.

Barnes' denial, and statement he has never spoken to Moore: Alan Wolfe, "Idiot Time," *New Republic* (July 8, 2002). See also Brit Hume, "Arafat's Power Still Strong," Fox News (April 12, 2002). Available from www.foxnews.com/story/0%2C2933%2C50152%2C00.html.

Moore's argument that the Nader campaign elected Senator Cantwell and thus forced a tie in Senate: Moore, *Stupid White Men,* p. 239.

Moore's claim that Pentagon budgeted $250 billion in 2000 for one aircraft: Ibid. p. 170.

Fritz debunks his claim: Ben Fritz, "One Moore Stupid White Man," *Spinsanity.com* (April 3, 2002). Available from www.spinsanity.org/columns/20020403.html.

Moore's claim that North Korean dictator Kim Jong Il is straightening out: Moore, *Stupid White Men,* p. 192.

North Korea's threat to Bush administration: David Sanger, "North Korea Says It Has Made Fuel for Atom Bombs," *New York Times* (July 15, 2003).

Moore attacks Cheney for being slow to sell Halliburton stock: "Idiot Time," Wolfe.

NOTES AND SOURCES

The *Post* attacks Cheney for selling Halliburton stock: Dana Milbank, "For Cheney, Tarnish from Halliburton," *Washington Post* (July 16, 2002), p. A1.

The *Post*'s earlier call for Cheney to sell: *Washington Post* [Editorial] (August 18, 2000), p. A42.

Moore's attack on Katherine Harris for purging felons from voter rosters: Moore, *Stupid White Men*, pp. 3, 4.

The stories on 1997 Miami election scandals include: State and Wire Reports, "State Voter Rolls: Election Official Finds More than 50,000 felons, 18,000 Dead Registered," *Panama City News Herald* (August 19, 1998). Available from www.newsherald.com/archive/local/ld081998.htm.

That the Florida Legislature appropriated $4 million to resolve problems: Scott Hiaasen, Gary Kane, and Elliot Jaspin, "Felon Purge Sacrificed Innocent Voters," *Palm Beach Post* (May 27, 2001). Available from www.commondreams.org/headlines01/0527-03.htm.

Moore claims 31 percent of black males in Florida are convicted felons: Moore, *Stupid White Men*, p. 4.

Greg Pelast puts the figure at 3 percent: Greg Palast, "The Great Florida Ex-Con Game: How the Felon Voter-Purge Was Itself Felonious," *Harper's* (March 1, 2002). Available from www.gregpalast.com/detail.cfm?artid=122&row=1.

The State's appellate process, through which 2,500 determinations that the voter was a felon were changed: Hiaasen, Kane, and Jaspin, op. cit.

The report that electoral officials in Democratic counties allowed felons to vote; at least 470 did so: David Kidwell and Lisa Arthur, "At Least 39 Felons Cast Illegal Votes," *Miami Herald* (November 18, 2000). Available from www.kressworks.com/Politics/Election_2000/Results/At_least_39_felons_cast_illegal_votes.htm.

Moore's description of high school being sadistic punishment and a totalitarian state: Moore, *Stupid White Men*, p. 97.

Moore on school being totalitarian: Ibid., p. 115.

Moore on face-slapping of teachers: Ibid., p. 102.

Moore discusses his former principal's decency and refers to winning the school board election: Ibid., p. 100.

Moore on his election and stoner vote: Ibid., p. 100.

Don Hammond describes Moore picking at toes and calling school board bums; Shawn Windsor and Marsha Low, "Moore Missing from Hall of Fame," *Detroit Free Press* (January 14, 2005), online at http://www.freep.com/entertainment/movies/moore14e_20050114 .htm.

"Helping MY BABY" grow quote: Ibid., p. 101.

The suggestions to sue the schools: Ibid., pp. 117–18.

Moore's list of alleged Bush transgressions: Ibid., pp. 164–65.

Moore's version of his October 23, 2000 speech at University of Florida, alleging that he said Florida Green Party members might have to vote for Democratic candidate Al Gore: Ibid., pp. 164–174.

Moore's October 20, 2000 attack on Sen Lieberman, Gore's running mate: Available from www.michaelmoore.com/words/ message/index.php?messageDate=2000-10-20÷. Incidentally, Moore's post-election appraisal of Lieberman indicates no change: "I think Lieberman's politics and campaign contributions are appalling." See www.michaelmoore.com/words/message/index.php? messageDate=2000-11-10.

Stephen I. Weiss's research into Moore's speech at the University of Florida: Available from www.iatribe.blogspot.com/2004_03_28_ iatribe_archive.html#108080419324993882.

SEARCHING FOR TRUTH IN *BOWLING FOR COLUMBINE*

Charlton Heston's and Wayne LaPierre's references to convention at Denver being cut to minimum: Kevin Flynn, "NRA Curtails Convention," *Rocky Mountain News* (April 22, 1999). Available from www.denver.rockymountainnews.com/shooting/0422nra3.shtml.

Heston's use of "cold, dead hands" in 2000: "Heston Addresses NRA: Gore Huge Threat to Our Second Amendment Rights," Associated

Press (May 21, 2000). Available from www.sipl.addr.com/nraheston. html.

Gore, Heston, and Jesse Jackson in Flint to campaign: Patricia Montemurri, "State Is Ground Zero, and Candidates Know It," *Detroit Free Press* (October 18, 2000). Available from www.freep. com/news/politics/zero18_20001018.htm.

The review stating incorrectly that Heston staged the rally within 48 hours of Kayla's death: Availble from www.highbeam.com/ library/doc0.asp?DOCID=1P1:70186632&refid=ip_almanac_hf and www.angela.byersworks.com/column/nov02.htm.

The review saying that Heston gave a speech immediately after her death: Angela C. Byers, "Voice of an Angel," online at www. geocities.com/youth4sa/columbine.html.

Moore's concession that Heston's visit was long after the girl's death: Clive Davis, "Not So Stupid White Men Fight Back," *Times of London* (June 18, 2003), p. 5.

Description of Heston's tour as nine stops in three states: NRA Fax Alert (October 10, 2000). Available from www.nrawinningteam. com/0010/tour.html.

Reviewer says Heston is an idiot and a racist: Rose Helin and Adam Ritscher, "Bowling 4 Columbine," online at www.geocities. com/youth4sa/columbine.html.

Reference to Heston leading actors' segment of Martin Luther King's march: Henry Levy, "CORE's Martin Luther King Jr. Annual Awards Dinner," available online at www.jewishpost.com/jp0703/ jpbr0703a.htm.

Moore was, by 1997, a resident of New York City: Daniel Radosh, "Moore Is Less," *Salon* (June 6, 1997). ("Instead He Got a $1.27 Million Apartment on the Upper West Side of Manhattan. You Didn't Think He Still Lived in Flint, Did You?" Available from www.salon. com/june97/media/media970606.html.

Federal restrictions on the sale of firearms to nonresidents of the dealer's state: 18 U.S. Code § 922(b)(3). (Incidentally, *only* licensed dealers have the power to sell to a nonresident.) New York

NOTES AND SOURCES

City rifle permit requirements are taken from the New York City Administrative Code § 10-303.: NY Admin. Code sec. 10-303. Available from www.atf.gov/firearms/statelaws/22edition.htm.

Technically, if Moore was a nonresident, he would only break the law (1) if he provided false ID or (2) took the rifle back to his home. However, Moore has stated that he took the rifle home. "I still do have that gun that I got at the bank. My wife is very upset. She wants it out of the house." Mikita Brottman, "Guns & Moses: An Interview with Filmmaker & Satirist Michael Moore." Available from https://securehost2.zen.co.uk/headpress/showroominfo.asp?ID=50#Excerpt.

Moore's splicing together of Willie Horton ads: Ben Fritz, "In *Bowling for Columbine,* Michael Moore Once Again Puts Distortions and Contradictions before the Truth," *Spinsanity* (November 19, 2002). Available from www.spinsanity.org/columns/20021119.html.

Moore's re-insertion of the Willie Horton ad in DVD version of *Bowling,* and his changing of the caption: Brendan Nyhan, "Moore Alters *Bowling* DVD in Response to Criticism," *Spinsanity* (September 3, 2003). Available from www.spinsanity.org/post.html?2003_08_31_archive.html.

Moore's wacko attacko's page talks about editing of the ad: Michael Moore, "How to Deal with the Lies and the Lying Liars When They Lie About *Bowling for Columbine.*" Available from www.michaelmoore.com/words/wackoattacko/index.php.

Documentation that Kayla's killer had fought with her, stabbed a student with a pencil, and later stabbed another one with a knife: Bill Bickel, "Murder in the First Grade." Available from www.crime.about.com/library/blfiles/blfirstgrade.htm; and David Kopel, "*Bowling* Truths," *National Review Online* (April 4, 2003). Available from www.nationalreview.com/kopel/kopel040403.asp.

Gun was stolen, bought by uncle for drugs: Violence Policy Center, "Where'd They Get Their Guns?" Available from www.vpc.org/studies/wgun000229.htm.

Moore acknowledges that Kayla's killer has since stabbed another child: Andrew Collins, "Michael Moore: Part II," *Guardian*

NOTES AND SOURCES

(November 11, 2002). Available from www.film.guardian.co.uk/ print/0,3858,4547674-101730,00.html.

The imprisonment of her killer's father: Bill Bickel, "Murder in the First Grade." Available from www.crime.about.com/library/blfiles/ blfirstgrade.htm.

The arrest of the killer's aunt and grandmother for drug dealing: Sheryl Janes, "Kayla's Death: Mourners Look Back and Move Forward," *Detroit Free Press* (February 28, 2001). Available from www. freep.com/news/metro/beech28_20010228.htm.

The father's reference to his son as being angry and the police officer's statement that the killer went from the hospital to the crack house: CBS News, March 7, 2000. Available from www.cbsnews. com/stories/2000/03/07/60II/main168970.shtml.

Gore, Heston, and Jesse Jackson's October 2000 presence in Flint to campaign is taken from Patricia Montemurri, "State Is Ground Zero, and Candidates Know It," *Detroit Free Press* (October 18, 2000). Available from www.freep.com/news/politics/zero18_ 20001018.htm.

Kayla Rolland was fatally shot on February 29, 2000, eight months before: Available from www.highbeam.com/library/doc0.asp?DOCID= 1P1:70186632&refid=ip_almanac_hf.

Data on the Lockheed plant's conversion of former nuclear-tipped missiles into civilian launchers: Lockheed's company web site: www.ast.lmco.com/launch_titanIIfacts.shtml.

Moore's wacko attacko letter about Lockheed: www.michaelmoore. com/words/wackoattacko/index.php.

The Lockheed plant spokesman's statement that he told Moore the plant makes no weapons: Clive Davis, "Not So Stupid White Men Fight Back," *Times of London* (June 18, 2003), p. 5.

That the National Rifle Association was founded by Union officers, via act of New York legislature: Jefferey Rodengen, *NRA: An American Legend* (Ft. Lauderdale, FL: Write Stuff Enterprises, 2002), pp. 17–18.

President Grant's crackdown on the Klan, arresting 5,000: "The Rise and Fall of Jim Crow," Public Broadcasting System, available from www.pbs.org/wnet/jimcrow/stories_events_enforce.html. Praise for him from Frederick Douglass and Douglass' friends also found online in this article.

Grant became NRA's eighth president: Rodengen, op. cit., p. 35.

General Sheridan's crackdown on the Klan and removal of governors who failed to suppress it: "War, Ruin, and Reconstruction Part II, 1866–1876", Texas State Library, online at www.tsl.state.tx.us/governors/war/page2.html.

The experience of Blacks who organized NRA chapters to defend themselves: Dr. Michael S. Brown, "Negroes with Guns," online at www.keepandbeararms.com/information/XcIBPrintItem.asp?ID=2960.

Moore's distortion of humanitarian aid to Afghanistan: Ben Fritz, "Viewer Beware," *Spinsanity* (November 19, 2002). Available from www.spinsanity.org/columns/20021119.html.

FBI figures on homicides: Available from FBI's Uniform Crime Reports, http://www.fbi.gov/ucr/01cius.htm; Centers for Disease Control 1999 homicide figures available from http://www.cdc.gov/nchs/releases/01facts/99mortality.htm. The 2001 FBI Report gives gun homicide figures as 8,719 in 2001, 8,661 in 2000, 8,480 in 1999 (p. 23).

Moore's statement that he used the 1999 Centers for Disease Control figures: "The U.S. figure of 11,127 Gun Deaths Comes from a Report from the Center for Disease Control." Available from http://www.michaelmoore.com/words/wackoattacko/index.php.

Comparative international figures on homicide: Available from www.nationmaster.com/graph-T/cri_mur_cap. Figures on rape: www.nationmaster.com/graph-T/cri_rap_cap.

Kleck and Gertz survey of defensive gun uses: Gary Kleck and Marc Gertz, "Armed Resistance to Crime," *Journal of Criminal Law and Criminology,* vol. 86, p.150 (1995). As to the higher use by women and minorities, their survey found that 16 percent of defensive gun uses over the previous five years were by Blacks and 46 percent by women, although the former are a minority and both reported lower than average gun ownership rates.

Swiss armament and low crime rates: "Switzerland and the Gun," BBC News (September 27, 2001). Available from www.news.bbc.co.uk/1/hi/world/europe/1566715.stm.

The best study of the role of Swiss firearms ownership and training on Nazi/Swiss relations: Stephen Halbrook, *Target Switzerland*, (Rockland City, NY: Sarpedon, 1998). Available from www.davekopel.org/2A/Mags/TargetSwitzerland.htm.

Swiss had 69 homicides in 2000: Available from www.nationmaster.com/country/sz/Crime.

Moore add-on DVD and references to bomber's plaque boasting that it killed thousands: Ben Fritz, "Moore alters *Bowling* DVD in response to criticism," September 2, 2003. Available online at www.spinsanity.org/post.html?2003_08_31_archive.html#10624779059990811.

Mike Pesca's interview of Michigan authorities, showing no evidence hunter had a videocamera: Available from www.wnyc.org/onthemedia/transcripts/transcripts_120602_more.html.

Discussion schoolyard shootings: Barry Glassner, *The Culture of Fear* (New York: Basic Books, 1999), pp. xiii-xv and 68–72. Glassner points out that in the average year, eight out of ten U.S. counties go without a single juvenile homicide, whether committed at school or elsewhere.

Glassner reference on three times as likely to be killed by lightning as by school violence: Ibid. p. xv.

Moore admits you are twice as likely to be killed by lightning as by school shooting: Michael Moore, *Stupid White Men* (New York: HarperCollins, 2002), p. 108.

MOORE MONEY

Bowling's gross is put at $55 million: Michael Skovmand, "Bowling for Columbine: I Want Them to Leave Angry," P.O.V. Available from www.imv.au.dk/publikationer/pov/Issue 16/section_1/artc3A.html.

Moore comments on taking money from "working stiffs": Available from Daniel Radosh, "Moore Is Less," *Salon* (June 6, 1997). Available from www.imv.au.dk/publikationer/pov/Issue_16/section_1/artc3A.html and www.salon.com/june97/media/media970606.html.

Moore's $1.9 million apartment in New York City: Available from www.us.imdb.com/name/nm0601619/bio.

Moore's $1.2 million house on Torch Lake, and beachfront problems: Shawn Windsor, "Prelude to the Academy Awards: The Many Roles of Michael Moore," *Detroit Free Press* (February, 28, 2004). Available from www.freep.com/entertainment/movies/moore28_20040228.htm.

Moore comments on taking money from "working stiffs": Daniel Radosh, "Moore Is Less," *Salon* (June 6, 1997). Available from www.salon.com/june97/media/media970606.html.

Moore discusses his minivan: Michael Moore, *Stupid White Men* (New York: HarperCollins, 2002), p. 121.

Moore's use of private jets, SUVs, and bodyguards is criticized in editorial: "Bowling for Credibility," *San Francisco Chronicle* [Editorial] (October 30, 2003), p. A-24. Available from www.sfgate.com/cgibin/article.cgi?file=/chronicle/archive/2003/10/30/EDG0R2LB101.DTL.

Moore's $5,200-per-day hotel room and his "me, me, me" speeches: Dixie Reid, "I'm Trying to Connect the Dots," *Sacramento Bee* (October 25, 2002). Available from www.bowlingforcolumbine.com/reviews/2002-10-25-sacra.php.

Moore charges Cornell $10,000 for speech: Linda Grace-Kobas, "Michael Moore Rips the Rich and Praises a 'Hero' Librarian," *Cornell Chronicle* (April 11, 2002). Available from www.news.cornell.edu/Chronicle/02/4.11.02/Michael_Moore.html.

His charging the University of Texas $25,000: "Moore, who bashed Bush at Oslans, charms UT crowd," Jeffrey Gilbert, *Austin American Statesman,* Tuesday, April 15, 2003.

The $30,000 tab for Kansas University: Mike Rigg, "Possible Moore Visit Inspires Awe in Some, Anger in Others at KU," *Lawrence Journal-World* (October 30, 2003). Available from www.ljworld.com/section/frontpage/story/150369.

Ann Kechner's refusal to attend the presentation of *Bowling* after discovering parents and survivors would be charged for tickets: Discussed in her letter to the editor *Rocky Mountain News* (October 18, 2003). Available from www.freerepublic.com/focus/f-news/1008341/posts.

Moore discusses his refusal to buy General Motors automobiles: Moore, *Stupid White Men,* p. 123.

Moore's quotation about 12-cent-per-hour Chinese sweatshops making Disney products: Michael Moore, *Dude, Where's My Country?* (New York, NY: Warner Books, 2003), p. 123.

Disney subsidiary Miramax financing his next movie: "American Bigmouth," Ella Taylor, *LA Weekly,* March 5–11, 2004. Available from www.laweekly.com/ink/04/15/features-taylor.php.

Former employee Eric Zicklin on Moore's statement that if he paid union scale he'd have to fire someone: Larissa Macfarquhar, "The Populist," *New Yorker* (February 16, 24, 2004). Available from www.newyorker.com/fact/content/?040216fa_fact7.

Moore's quotation on capitalism as an evil empire: "Michael Moore's ongoing crusade against corporate greed won him an audience with big, bad Nike," Ian Hodden, online at www.industrycentral.net/director_interviews/MM02.HTM.

Moore boasts of being multimillionaire: Tim Blair, "Moore Is Less," Fox News (March 22, 2002). Available from www.foxnews.com/story/0%2C2933%2C48562%2C00.html.

Moore's quotation on how Flint newspaper and liberal New Yorkers are jealous of his apartment: "Michael Moore," Stephen Thompson,

The Onion AV Club, October 25, 2000. Online at www.theavclub. com/avclub3638/avfeature_3638.html.

Moore writes a letter to Elian Gonzalez: "A Letter of Apology to Elian Gonzalez from Michael Moore," *Michael Moore,* March 31, 2000. Online at www.michaelmoore.com/words/message/index. php?messageDate=2000-03-31.

TV Nation writers who have not been paid, noted in two sources: Rick Marin, "The Truth about Michael Moore," *Washington Times* (February 14, 1990), and available from www.salon.com/june97/ media/media970606.html.

MICHAEL MOORE'S LAST DAYS IN OFFICE

On page 217 of the hardcover first edition of *Stupid White Men,* Moore provides a list of orders enacted by President Clinton during his final weeks in office in late 2000 and early 2001.

Moore sued *Mother Jones* magazine and settled out of court for $58,000: Rick Marin, "The Truth about Michael Moore," *Washington Times* (February 14, 1990).

Moore carried a cardboard cutout of Saddam Hussein during his 2003 promotional tour for *Dude, Where's My Country?:* Reports of this are widely available, including: Paul Brownfield, "Biting the Hand That Flies Him," *Los Angeles Times* (October 27, 2003).

Moore's letter to Elian Gonzalez: Available from www.michaelmoore. com/words/message/index.php?messageDate=2000-03-31.

Moore reported on his web site that General Wesley Clark was contacted by the White House following September 11 and asked to spread rumors that Iraq had a hand in the tragedy: Available from www.michaelmoore.com/words/message/index.php?messageDate= 2003-09-23.

The assertions leveled by former employees of Moore's *TV Nation:* Daniel Radosh, "Moore Is Less," *Salon* (June 6, 1997).

DUDE, WHERE'S YOUR INTEGRITY?

Moore's eulogy to Bill Weems: Michael Moore, *Dude, Where's My Country?* (New York: Warner Books, 2003), p. x.

Moore's "scaredy cat" speech: Yasmin Alibhai-Brown, "Black on Black Violence: There Is a Way Forward," *Independent,* [Britain] (January 6, 2003). Available from www.argument.independent.co.uk/ regular_columnists/yasmin_alibhai_brown/story.jsp?story=36672 5 and www.obv.org.uk/reports/2003/rpt20030106e.htm.

Moore's comment that "many families have been devastated tonight" and that if hijackers meant to get back at Bush they should not have attacked areas that voted for Gore: Available from www. michaelmoore.com/words/message/index.php?messageDate=2001-09-12.

Moore asks why terrorists didn't target locations that voted for Bush: "Death, Downtown," Michael Moore, September 12, 2001. Initially appeared on his web site, removed shortly thereafter. Reproduced online at www.zmag.org/moorecalam.htm.

Moore's complaints of his publisher censoring him: Moore, *Dude,* p. xii.

Moore notes that Saudis have trillions invested in the United States: Ibid., p. 13.

Description of Saudi Arabia as a dictatorship: Ibid., p. 14.

Moore's whimsical description of lunatic dictator Kim Jong Il: Michael Moore, *Stupid White Men* (New York: HarperCollins, 2002), pp. 190–191.

Richard Clarke's statement that no bin Laden left until he cleared it with FBI: "Flights of Fancy," Barbara Mikkelson, March 31, 2004. Online at www.snopes.com/rumors/flight.htm.

Citing Bill Andrews: "Bin Laden Family's US Exit 'Approved,'" *Edinburgh Evening News* (September 3, 2003).

The Brady Act provision requiring destruction of records if gun purchaser is cleared by the system: 18 U.S. Code § 922(t)(2). The regulations forbidding access to the record system, except to enforce Federal firearms laws or review issuances of explosives and firearms permits can be found at 28 Code of Federal Regulations § 25.6(j). The regulations imposing a $10,000 fine for violation can be found at 28 Code of Federal Regulations § 25.11(3). The Code of Federal Regulations provisions are also found in the July 2000 edition, confirming that they date from the Clinton era.

Moore discusses the Taliban delegation's visit to the United States and mentions that its 1998 return was sponsored by State Department: Moore, *Dude*, p. 27.

President Clinton's references to Iraqi weapons of mass destruction are from CNN, February 17, 1998, online at www.cnn.com/ALLPOLITICS/1998/02/17/transcripts/clinton.iraq.

Senator Hillary Clinton's speech on Iraq: Available from www.clinton.senate.gov/~clinton/speeches/iraq_101002.html.

The terrorist summit meeting in Iran: Richard Miniter, *Losing bin Laden* (Washington, DC: Regnery, 2003) p. 106.

Miniter adds a large appendix outlining documented ties between al-Qaeda and Iraq: Ibid., pp. 231–41.

Al Qaeda and Hussein hate the United States for different reasons: Ibid., p. 238.

Iraq terrorist training camp: Delroy Murdock, "At Salman Pak," National Review Online (April 7, 2003). Available from www.nationalreview.com/murdock/murdock040703.asp.

Khoda's interview: Available from www.pbs.org/wgbh/pages/frontline/shows/gunning/interviews/khodada.html.

Syria seeking Australian intervention with the United States: John Kerrin, "Syria Seeks Our Help to Woo Us", *Australian* (March 27, 2004). Available from www.theaustralian.news.com.au/common/story_page/0,5744,9088802%255E601,00.html.

Libya admits to nuclear weapons, allows inspection: "Libya to Allow Weapons Inspections," Fox News (December 20 2003). Available from www.foxnews.com/story/0,2933,106263,00.html. "Libyan leader Moammar Gadhafi, in an exclusive interview with CNN, acknowledged Monday that the war in Iraq may have played a role in his decision to dismantle his country's weapons of mass destruction programs." "Gadhafi: Iraq War May Have Influenced WMD Decision," CNN News (December 22, 2003). Available from www.cnn.com/2003/WORLD/africa/12/22/gadhafi.interview/index.html.

Gaddafi's son's speech: Maamoun Youssef, "Gadhafi's Son: Bush Plan Should Be Backed," *Guardian Unlimited* (March 25, 2004). Available from www.guardian.co.uk/worldlatest/story/0,1280,-3900155,00.html.

Moore on need to end preemptive war: Moore, *Dude,* p. 125.

Moore on how the United States at present is like Germany during the rise of the Nazis: Byron York, "Of course They Think Bush Is a Nazi," *National Review Online* (January 7, 2003). Available from www.nationalreview.com/york/york200401070805.asp.

On how the United States is starting toward a police state and martial law: "Moore, the Merrier," October 11, 2003, Available from www.smh.com.au/articles/2003/10/10/1065676154259.html?from=storyrhs.

Moore on getting rid of guns: Phil Donahue interviews Michael Moore, "Michael Moore Unplugged," November 20, 2002. Available from www.alternet.org/story.html?StoryID=14589.

Moore lists Nixon as the last liberal president: Moore, *Dude,* p. 193. See also Edward Epstein, *Agency of Fear* (New York: Putnam, 1977) for an excellent study of Nixon's expansion of federal law enforcement.

Moore's pledge to contribute to Democrats: Moore, *Dude,* p. 162.

Moore statement that Democrats have written off 2004 and might as well run Oprah: Ibid., pp. 204, 206.

Moore's political contribution record can be verified on the Federal Election Commission online database at www.herndon1.sdrdc.com/fecimg/norindsea.html.

AND THE OSCAR FOR ACTING OUT GOES TO . . .

The authors would note an ironic feature of this chapter, in that we are responding to a suspected narcissist by . . . devoting an entire book to him.

The diagnostic definition of Narcissistic Personality Disorder is summarized from the American Psychiatric Association, *Diagnostic and Statistical Manual of Mental Disorders*, 4th ed., text rev. (Washington, D.C.: Author, 2000). Available from www.en. wikipedia.org/wiki/Narcissism.

Moore's boasts of wealth: Tim Blair, "Moore Is Less," Fox News (March 22, 2002). Available from www.foxnews.com/story/0%2C2933%2C48562%2C00.html.

The narcissist lectures rather than speaks: Sam Vaknin, *Malignant Self Love: Narcissism Revisited* (Prague, Czech Republic: Narcissus Publications, 2003).

Moore's hectoring letter to Al Gore: Michael Moore, "An Open Letter to Al Gore," online at www.michaelmoore.com/words/message/index.php?messageDate=2000-10-31.

Moore's call to Nader staff: "I spoke to the three people who were running his campaign, aware there was a chance the man himself was listening in." Michael Moore, *Stupid White Men* (New York: HarperCollins), p. 251.

Moore's plan to take over the NRA: Christopher Cobb, "Michael Moore Documentary Explores Media-Induced Fear," *Daily Bruin* [UCLA] (October 11, 2002). Available from www.uwire.com/content/topae101102002.html.

"I live on the island of Manhattan": Moore, *Stupid White Men*, p. 51.

Letter to Elian Gonzalez: Michael Moore, "Letter of Apology to Elian Gonzalez." Available from www.michaelmoore.com/words/message/index.php?messageDate=2000-03-31.

Moore's former agent fired him: Clive Davis, "Not So Stupid White Men Fight Back," *Times of London* (June 6, 2003), p. 5.

NOTES AND SOURCES

Former employee at *TV Nation* says she has to think of him as an entertainer: Larissa Macfarquhar, "The Populist," *New Yorker* (February 16, 24, 2004). Available from www.newyorker.com/fact/content/?040216fa_fact7.

Moore's rant against staff at the Roundhouse Theater: Page Six, "Disgrace of 'Stupid' Windbag," *New York Post* (January 8, 2003).

Narcissists desire to speak directly to authority figure: Vaknin, *Malignant Self Love*, p. 370.

Moore is superb in getting people to make idiots of themselves on camera. Daniel Radosh, "Moore Is Less," *Salon* (June 6, 1997). Available from www.groups.google.com/groups?selm=9nnsv5%2418mc%241%40pencil.math.missouri.edu&output=gplain.

Matt Stone and Moore's reactions to Heston's announcement of his Alzheimer's Disease and note that Moore won't quit when behind: "No Mercy for Stricken Heston," *New York Post* (October 21, 2002). Available from www.pqasb.pqarchiver.com/nypost/results.html?num=25&st=basic&QryTxt=%22Michael+Moore%22+heston+south+park&sortby=REVERSE_CHRON&datetype=7.

Moore describes how the Flint paper and New Yorkers are jealous of his apartment: Stephen Thompson, *The Onion AV Club*, Vol. 36, No. 38 (October 25, 2000). Online at www.theavclub.com/feature/index.php?issue=3638&f=1.

Envy is at the core of narcissist's personality: Vaknin, *Malignant Self Love*, p. 305. Available from www.samvak.tripod.com/faq67.html.

Moore lashes out at Matt Hirsch, upon his presenting Moore with oversized check: Shannon Brescher, "Moore Speaks Out About His Book, Life After Sept. 11," *Cornell Daily Sun* (April 4, 2002). Available from www.cornelldailysun.com/vnews/display.v/ART/2002/04/04/108143300540755badd4cd6?in_archive=1.

Moore's hint that former Representative Joe Scarborough might have murdered his aide: Larissa Macfarquhar, "The Populist," *New Yorker* (February 16, 24). Available from www.newyorker.com/fact/content/?040216fa_fact7 (posted February 9, 2004).

References to Moore reserving www.joescarboroughkilledhisintern.
com: Available from www.peelio.com/johnny/archives/2003_10.
html,www.216.239.57.104/search?q=cache:1LfVL7rsxEOJ:www.
niallmcloughlin.com/wblog/archives/cat_politics.html+%22michael+
moore%22+Klausutis&hl=en&ie=UTF-8 [cached] and www.
allhatnocattle.net/10-25-03_dubya_halloween.htm. An internet
search confirmed that the domain name is reserved, although the
location has no content.

Moore lashes out at small business during an interview with the
Arcata Eye: Available from www.arcataeye.com/top/020312top02.
shtml.

Moore has Alan Edelstein arrested for use of Moore-like tactics:
John Tierny, "When the Tables Turn, the Knives Come Out," *New
York Times.* Available from www.partners.nytimes.com/library/
national/regional/061700ny-col-tierney.html.

The narcissist's quest for martyrdom: Vaknin, *Malignant Self Love,*
p. 161. Available from www.samvak.tripod.com/faq56.html.

The janitor's statement that Moore said, "[T]here are people outside
who want to kill me": Peter Rowe, "Don't Judge an Author by His
Cover," *San Diego Union-Tribune* (March 19, 2002), p. E1.

Moore's account of the "police raid" of his San Diego book signing:
Available from www.sonoran-sunsets.com/stupid.html.

Kynn Bartlett's account of the police raid: Available from www.
kynn.com/politics/Moore.

FAHRENHEIT 9/11: THE TEMPERATURE AT WHICH TRUTH GOES TO HELL IN A HANDBASKET

Danny Goldberg, "Hollywood on Trial" *AlterNet* (November 23,
2004), online at http://www.alternet.org/election04/20567, cites
Nebraska Governor Mike Johanns as stating that every time Moore
endorsed Kerry, Kerry's numbers took a dive in his state.

Leon Panetta's "The party of FDR has become the party of Michael
Moore and that doesn't help the party": Ibid.

NOTES AND SOURCES

Moore's claim that Senator Daschle had attended a screening and "he gave me a hug and said he felt bad and that we were all gonna fight from now on. I thanked him for being a good sport" was covered by *Time* magazine and other sources. See "The World According to Michael: Taking Aim at George W., A Populist Agitator Makes Noise, News and a New Kind of Political Entertainment," *Time* (July 12, 2004), online at http://www.michaelmoore.com/words/latestnews/mikeinthenews/index.php?id=62.

Daschle's denial of the hugging (albeit with an admission he had attended the screening) was carried in the *Rapid City Journal*. See "Daschle Denies Hugging Moore," *Rapid City Journal* (July 8, 2004), online at http://www.rapidcityjournal.com/articles/2004/07/09/news/local/news05.txt.

Moore's producer's denial that Moore did not intend to create the impression that bin Ladens flew during no-fly ban is found in John Mintz, "No Impropriety Found in Saudis' Exit Flights," *Washington Post* (July 24, 2004), p. A11, online at http://www.washingtonpost.com/wp-dyn/articles/A10070-2004Jul23.html.

Secretary Rumsfeld's press conference, relating to negotiation of anti-terrorism agreements with the Philippines, is from Department of Defense, "DoD News Briefing—Secretary Rumsfeld and Gen. Myers" (February 28, 2003), online at http://www.defenselink.mil/transcripts/2003/t02282003_t0228sd.html.

President Bush's interview with MSNBC comes from *Meet the Press* (February 13, 2004), online at http://www.msnbc.msn.com/id/4179618.

Chairman Kean's statement that the 9/11 Commission had "wonderful access" to documents is from *Meet the Press* (July 25, 2004), online at http://www.msnbc.msn.com/id/5488345.

Bush administration in 2001 tried to use diplomacy to deal with bin Laden: *The 9/11 Commission Report* (New York: Norton, 2004), p. 203.

Bush administration told Taliban representative that it did not recognize the Taliban, and rejected its claims that it had complied with requests to isolate bin Laden: Thomas Frank, "Film Offers Limited View," *Newsday* (June 27, 2004), p. A.6, online at http://pqasb.pqarchiver.com/newsday/655767111.html?did=655767111& FMT=ABS&FMTS=FT&date=Jun+27%2C+2004&author=THOMAS+ FRANK&desc=ANALYSIS%2C+Film+offers+limited+view . Free edition online at http://moorewatch.com/index.php/a_limited_view.

Hamid Karzai's biography as an anti-Taliban leader can be found online at http://www.achievement.org/autodoc/page/kar0bio-1. Zalmay Khalizad's background is online at http://www.american-president.org/history/bushgeorgew/bushIIstaffadvisers/national-security/nationalsecuritycouncil/neareastandnorthafricanaffairs/zalmaykhalilzad/h_index.shtml.

Accusations that Moore's depictions of Arabs are racist can be found at http://www.tompaine.com/articles/blind_or_a_coward.php and http://counterpunch.org/jensen07052004.html.

President Bush's November 3, 2002, speech in Minnesota is online at http://www.vote-smart.org/speech_detail.php?speech_id=4613.

President Bush's September 21, 2001, speech to airline employees can be found online at http://www.whitehouse.gov/news/releases/2001/09/20010927-1.html.

Secretary of Defense Rumsfeld's March 4, 2003, speech to former members of Congress is online at http://www.findarticles.com/p/articles/mi_m0PAH/is_2003_March_4/ai_104438392.

Vice President Cheney's October 10, 2003, speech to the Heritage Foundation is online at http://www.whitehouse.gov/news/releases/2003/10/20031010-1.html.

Dr. Kelton Rhoads' paper, "Propaganda Tactics and *Fahrenheit 9/11*" can be found online at http://www.workingpsychology.com/download_folder/Propaganda_And_Fahrenheit.pdf.

The story of the Moore's rewriting of the *Pantagraph* letter to the editor is set out in full at http://moorewatch.com/index.php/weblog/just_the_fax_maam, complete with images of the real letter to the editor and of Moore's supposed headline.

NOTES AND SOURCES

9/11 Commission report takes Moore to pieces: *9/11 Commission Report,* pp. 329–330.

Richard Clarke takes responsibility for evacuating the Saudis: Alexander Bolton, "Clarke Claims Responsibility on The Hill" (May 26, 2004), online at http://www.thehill.com/news/052604/clarke.aspx. Clarke's statement to AP: "Richard Clarke: Big Part of Moore's Movie 'a Mistake,'" *Newsmax* (June 30, 2004), online at http://www.newsmax.com/archives/ic/2004/7/1/00111.shtml.

Moore spokesman says that he did not intend to create the impression that the Saudis were evacuated during the ban on flying is found in John Mintz, "No Impropriety Found in Saudis' Exit Flights," *Washington Post* (July 24, 2004), p. A11, online at http://www.washingtonpost.com/wp-dyn/articles/A10070-2004Jul23.html.

Moore's reference to James Bath and Arbusto: Michael Moore, *Dude, Where's My Country?* (New York, NY: Warner Books, 2003), p. 6.

Unger repudiates Bath/Bush/bin Laden link: Craig Unger, *House of Bush, House of Saud* (New York: Charles Scribner's Sons, 2004) p. 101.

Moore citation of New York times story: Moore, *Dude,* p. 4.

Moore's spin on the evacuation of bin Ladens: Ibid., pp. 20, 21.

A more complete version of the *New York Times* story: Patrick E. Tyler, "Fearing Harm, bin Laden Kin Fled from U.S.," *New York Times* (September 30, 2001). Available from www.cndyorks.gn.apc.org/news/articles/binladenfamily.htm.

Moore's *Playboy* Interviews: Rob Walton, "Crude Awakening," available online at www.playboy.com/arts-entertainment/features/michaelmoore/index.html.

Whether a flight occurred on September 13 is still disputed; Bodyguard Dan Grossi asserts that a flight occurred on September 13, which the FBI and FAA deny: Kathy Steele and William March, "Probe Revisits Saudis' 'Phantom Flight,'" *Tampa Tribune* (March 26, 2004), p. 1.

September 15 and 16 flights: Craig Unger posted the manifest for the flights on his webpage. Available from www.houseofbush. com/files.php.

FBI interviewed Saudis and checked baggage and watch lists: Steele and March, "Probe Revisits Saudis' 'Phantom Flight'." This is a contradiction to Unger's statement that the FBI was asked to interview the Saudis and did not. Unger, *House of Bush, House of Saud,* pp. 12, 257, 259. It is possible that Unger's sources, mostly airport officials, were not told that the FBI had interviewed the Saudis.

Dale Watson authorized flight: Patrik E. Tyler, op. cit.

The Carlyle Group web site indicates it manages 18 billion dollars: Available from www.thecarlylegroup.com/eng/company/l3-company732.html.

The Carlyle Group has $100 million in Soros investments: Oliver Burkeman and Julian Borger, "The Ex-Presidents' Club," *Guardian* [United Kingdom] (October 31, 2000). Available from www.guardian. co.uk/wtccrash/story/0%2C1300%2C583869%2C00.html. and www. mindfully.org/WTO/2003/George-Soros-Statesman2jun03.htm.

Briody's appraisal of Soros' role in building the Carlyle Group: Dan Briody, *The Iron Triangle: Inside the Secret World of the Carlyle Group* (John Wiley & Sons, 2003), pp. 84–85.

Moore states he had sensational prisoner abuse footage and held it back: Ruthe Stein, "Documentarian Kept Quiet After Filming U.S. Soldiers Abusing Iraqis," *San Francisco Chronicle* (June 13, 2004), online at http://www.sfgate.com/cgi-bin/article.cgi?file=/c/a/2004/06/13/MNG2K75D7S1.DTL&type=printable.

Moore tells *New York Times* he might reveal some footage: Jim Rutenberg, "A Film to Polarize Along Party Lines," *New York Times* (May 17, 2004), p. E-1, online at http://query.nytimes.com/search/restricted/article?res=F30913FF3F5B0C748DDDAC0894DC404482.

Moore admits Iraqi "corpse" was actually an unconscious drunk: Liam Lacey, "Call It Gunning for Dubya," (May 18, 2004), p. R1, online at http://www.theglobeandmail.com/servlet/Page/document/

v4/sub/MarketingPage?user_URL=http://www.theglobeandmail.co
m%2Fservlet%2FArticleNews%2FTPStory%2FLAC%2F20040518%
2FCANNES18%2FTPEntertainment%2FFilm&ord=1107124952744
&brand=theglobeandmail&force_login=true. A free version is online
at http://www.20six.co.uk/weblogEntry/51lpxzn19gqz.htm. See
also Ian Youngs, "Moore Film Shows 'US Iraqi Abuse,'" *BBC News*
(May 17, 2004), online at http://news.bbc.co.uk/2/hi/entertain-
ment/3720569.stm.

John Kerry's speech claiming that Bush "outsourced" the attempt
to capture bin Laden at Tora Bora can be found at http://www.
thinkthevote.com/news.asp?ID=1261. A similar Kerry remark can
be found at http://www.indepundit.com/archive2/2004/10/
general_kerry_1.html.

General Franks' response to Kerry's charges is from Tommy Franks,
"War of Words," *New York Times* (October 19, 2004), p. A-27.

Hundreds of Taliban died at Tora Bora, and no American lives were
lost: Melanie Kirkpatrick, "Tora Bora Baloney," *Wall Street Journal
Online* (October 14, 2004), online at http://www.opinionjournal.
com/editorial/feature.html?id=110005754.

Moore's version of a plot to get a pipeline for Unocal through
Afghanistan and speculation as to Bush's involvement: Michael
Moore, *Dude, Where's My Country* (New York: Warner Books, 2003),
pp. 27–29.

Clinton officials touting of the Unocal pipeline through Afghanistan: Craig Rosebraugh, "Don't Mess with Unocal," online at
www.thirdworldtraveler.com/central_Asia_watch/Don't%20Mess_
Unocal.html; "Corporations, National Security, and War Profiteering," *Multinational Monitor*, Vol. 22, No. 11 (November 2001),
online at multinationalmonitor.org/mm2001/01november/
nov01interviewrashid.html.

Unocal contributes to the Democractic Party: Jennifer Shecter,
"Money in Politics Alert," *Open Secrets*, Vol. 3, No. 45 (December 8,
1997). Online at www.opensecrets.org/alerts/v3/ALRTV3N45.asp.

NOTES AND SOURCES

The Clinton Administration conduct with regard to Sudan is thoroughly criticized: Gerald Posner, "I Was Wrong about Bush," *Wall Street Journal* (September 25, 2001), pp. 101–104, available from www.posner.com/I_Was_Wrong_About_Bush.htm; and Mansoor Ijaz, "Clinton Let Bin Laden Slip Away and Metastasize," *Los Angeles Times* (December 5, 2001), p. B.13.

The decision of Miramax, a Disney subsidiary, to fund *Fahrenheit 9/11:* Ella Taylor, "American Bigmouth: Why Michael Moore Won't Shut up," *L.A. Weekly* (March 5–11, 2004). Available from www.laweekly.com/ink/04/15/features-taylor.php.

Disney's use of third-world sweatshops to produce shirts and cartoon-related trinkets has been extensively criticized: Available from www.cleanclothes.org/companies/disney.htm; www.nlcnet.org/campaigns/shahmakhdum/; and www.maquilasolidarity.org/campaigns/disney/report.htm.

Moore's reference to Miramax investing $6 million in his film: Michael Moore, "When You Wish Upon a Star," online at www.alternet.org/story.html?StoryID=18646.

The Xenel contract and alleged ties to bin Laden: April Hunt, "Chamber Tells Osceola County, Fla., Officials to Sign Builder," *Orlando Sentinel* (December 7, 2002). Available from www.pqasb.pqarchiver.com/orlandosentinel/256241061.html?did=256241061&FMT=ABS&FMTS=FT&date=Dec+7,+2002&author=April+Hunt,+Sentinel+Staff+Writer&desc=CHAMBER+TELLS+OSCEOLA+TO+SIGN+BUILDER,+IGNORE+TERRORIST+LINKS and www.enr.com/news/otherSources/2002/12/07/krtbn/0000-0298-OR-BUILDER.asp.

Carlyle Group and bin Talal ties to Disney: Available from www.disinfopedia.org/wiki.phtml?title=Carlyle_Group.

Soros expenditures against Bush: Laura Blumenfeld, "Billionaire Soros Takes on Bush," *Washington Post* (November 11, 2003), p. A3.

In *Dude, Where's My Country?*, Moore unveils what he sees as a plot. *Dude, Where's My Country?*, pp. 27–35. For Disney and Carlyle: www.disinfopedia.org/wiki.phtml?title=Carlyle_Group.

Moore knew nearly a year in advance that Miramax/Disney would not distribute *Fahrenheit 9/11:* "Moore Than a Movie?" *Washington Dispatch,* May 18, 2004, online at http://www.washingtondispatch. com/sportsbar/archives/000224.html.

On May 17, 2004, *CNS News* reported that the deal between Miramax's owners and Disney was already made. David Thibault, "Michael Moore's Anti-Bush Film May Reach Public in July" *CNS News,* May 17, 2004 online at http://www.cnsnews.com/ViewPolitics. asp?Page=%5CPolitics%5Carchive%5C200405%5CPOL20040517b. html. ("Michael Moore's latest film with an attitude, may end up in. American movie theaters as soon as July, following the deal reached between Miramax Films . . . and Miramax's corporate parent, the Walt Disney Co. . . . Bob and Harvey Weinstein, co-chief executives of Miramax, will acquire the rights to the movie and find a new distributor.")

On May 18, the *Washington Post* was still breaking the news that "Bob and Harvey Weinstein, who head Disney-owned Miramax Pictures, are currently in negotiations with Disney to buy the film . . ." and the *Montreal Gazette* was telling readers that "Miramax bosses Harvey and Bob Weinstein are trying to buy back the film and find another distributor . . .": Desson Thomson, "'Fahrenheit 9/11': Connecting With a Hard Left," *Washington Post,* May 18, 2004, p. C1, online at http://www.washingtonpost.com/wp-dyn/articles/ A34917-2004May17.html; David Germain, "Fahrenheit 9/11 Fires Up Audiences at Cannes," *Montreal Gazette,* May 18, 2004, online at http://www.canada.com/montreal/montrealgazette/news/arts/ story.html?id=cf88f78c-3b5f-4931-9fad-ad21c9af26ee.

MOORE AND TERRORISM

9/11 hijacker Mohamed Atta received a master's degree from the University of Hamburg: Lorraine Passchier, "Anatomy of a Suicide Hijacker," *CTV News.* Available from www.popups.ctv.ca/content/ publish/popups/war_on_terror/network_of_terror/global_network/ anatomy.htm.

NOTES AND SOURCES

That five other of the hijackers attended Hamburg: Gerald Posner, *Why America Slept* (New York: Random House, 2003), p. 159n; "The Recruiters," *CBC News* (March 16, 2004), available from www.cbc.ca/national/news/recruiters/moussaoui.html; and *BBC News*, "Atta trained in Afghanistan," available from www.news.bbc. co.uk/1/hi/world/americas/2213701.stm

That Moussaoui, the alleged twentieth hijacker, received his bachelor's degree in France and his master's degree in the United Kingdom: Available from www.fas.org/irp/world/para/docs/mous_indict.html.

Franz Fanon's most popular work was *The Wretched of the Earth*, (New York, NY: Grove Press, 1963). Fanon, by training a psychiatrist, argued that oppressed colonials would of necessity be in spiritual bondage to the West: Even if liberated, they would still see themselves as inferiors. Only by fighting would they free themselves of the psychic shackles; ethnic differences would disappear under this liberation.

Sure. In practice, Fanon was a recipe for civil war and ethnic cleansing. But Fanon's ideas *sounded* great at the time. Revolutionaries had always known that shooting people and blowing things up was better sport than pushing a plow and staring at a water buffalo's posterior. Now there was no reason to feel guilty about it. It wasn't just goofing off and committing atrocities—it was a moral and psychic imperative.

The Western origins of Qutbism: John Gray, "How Marx Turned Muslim," *Independent* [UK] (July 27, 2002). Available from www. enjoyment.independent.co.uk/books/reviews/story.jsp?story=318696.

Sayyid Qutb's education and travels: Available from www.salaam. co.uk/knowledge/biography/viewentry.php?id=1365.

Qutbism's roots in Marx: Daniel Pipes, "The Western Mind of Modern Islam," *First Things* (December 1995), available from www. danielpipes.org/article/273; and Paul Berman, "The Philosopher of Islamic Terror," *New York Times* (March 23, 2003). Available from www.nytimes.com/2003/03/23/magazine/23GURU.html?ex=1081742400&en=970d993af7276bee&ei=5070.

NOTES AND SOURCES

Background of Islamic Jihad leadership: Pipes, "The Western Mind of Modern Islam."

Qutb's dislike of America: "All Things Considered," *National Public Radio* (May 6, 2003). Available from www.npr.org/display_pages/features/feature_1253796.html.

Moore's description of Iraqi insurgents as minutemen and revolutionaries: "Michael Moore's comments on Bush's A13 News Conference," Friday, April 16, 2004, online at www.thunderbay.indymedia.org/news/2004/04/13497.php.

Moore's claim that the United States created bin Laden: "Mike's letter of September 12, 2001," on his web site at www.michaelmoore.com/words/message/index.php?messageDate=2001-09-12.

"[W]e have orphaned so many": www.michaelmoore.com/words/message/index.php?messageDate=2001-09-12.

U.S. is culpable in so many acts of terror: Michael Moore, "Somewhere in the Land of Enchantment," online at www.michaelmoore.com/words/message/index.php?messageDate=2001-09-15.

Tale of F-16 chasing aircraft that hit the World Trade Center: Available from www.michaelmoore.com/words/message/index.php?messageDate=2001-09-15.

The Bali bomber's defense counsel's quotation of Michael Moore, and the bombers aim at "lots of whiteys": Richard S. Ehrlich, "Bali Bomber Imam Samudra Welcomed Death Call," available from www.scoop.co.nz/mason/stories/HL0308/S00100.htm; and Darren Goodsir, "Infidels Had Bali Coming, Not That I Did It, Says Samudra," *Sydney Morning Herald* (August 12, 2003), available from www.smh.com.au/articles/2003/08/11/1060588323997.html.

The translation of bin Laden's 2004 videotape can be found at "Full Transcript of Bin Laden's Speech," *Al-Jazeera* (November 1, 2004), online at http://english.aljazeera.net/NR/exeres/79C6AF22-98FB-4A1C-B21F-2BC36E87F61F.htm.

Moore's post-9/11 complaint that the terrorists had targeted places that voted against Bush has been removed from his webpage, but can still be found at sites such as http://groups-beta.google.

NOTES AND SOURCES

com/group/misc.activism.progressive/msg/66c4e3ad1ef3b880?q=%22places+that+voted+AGAINST+Bush%22&hl=en&lr=&ie=UTF-8&safe=off&rnum=7.

The Middle East Media Research Project translation of bin Laden's speech can be found online at http://www.memritv.org/Transcript.asp?P1=312.

Yigal Carmon's article is "Osama vs. Bush," *National Review Online* (October 31, 2004), http://www.nationalreview.com/document/carmon200410311937.asp.

MOORE STORIES

Quotes and information on the film *Michael Moore Hates America* are culled from a telephone interview with Michael Wilson conducted on April 13, 2004. Additional information is taken from various "Filmmaker's Journal" reports written by Michael Wilson during 2003/2004, from his web site, www.michaelmoorehatesamerica.com, and from various published reports.

CLOSING THOUGHTS

Moore's "How can there be inaccuracy in comedy?" defense: Michelle Cottle, "Moore Is Less," *New Republic*. Available from www.tnr.com/doc.mhtml?i=life&s=cottle050704 (posted May 7, 2004).

Reports of health care companies warning their employees about Moore, and rumors that Moore hired actors to portray health care professionals taken from Elaine Dutka, "Giving Them a Sick Feeling: Drug Firms Are on the Defense as Filmmaker Michael Moore Plans to Dissect Their Industry," *Los Angeles Times* (December 22, 2004).

AUTHORS' ACKNOWLEDGMENTS

I'd first like to acknowledge some people who played key roles in giving me my latest obsession. Dan Gifford, producer (with Mike McNulty) of the Oscar-nominated documentary, "Waco: The Rules of Engagement" first mentioned Moore and *Bowling for Columbine* to me, with the suggestion that it was a pity no one had examined this supposed documentary. Much followed from that casual suggestion. Aid and example came from Jim Kennefick over at moorewatch.com.

There are also the thousands of people (literally: At one point the count was 200 a day) who have sent me e-mails relating to Moore, tipping me to this or that event, or contributing ideas and insights. The theme of narcissism owes much to my buddy Bill Bailey; insights into Moore's video techniques come from several video producers who tipped me to camera angles and techniques.

Special thanks for the tolerance shown by my spouse Victoria Hardy, and the kids—Mark, Madelyn, and Nathaniel Hardy, and Emily and Nevin Kuser.

DAVID T. HARDY

AUTHORS' ACKNOWLEDGMENTS

To the thousands of Americans who have stood up and made something of Moorelies.com over the past year, heartfelt and grateful thanks are due. Your tips, your letters, and your involvement have all been vital to the public awareness campaign we've waged together.

In creating this book, several people are owed many thanks. Bridie Clark truly is due the credit for making this book a reality. I will not forget her long-hand note taking and her friendship. Others I'm grateful to at HarperCollins are Judith Regan, for standing up and giving voice to a cause; Jennifer Suitor; Daniel Nayeri; and the copy, legal, and research departments.

Special thanks are due to Shawn for getting Moorelies.com up and keeping it running smoothly, and for his wisdom in matters technical and otherwise over the years. Thanks are also due to Joe, Anthony, Stuart, and Henry.

Finally, thank you to the parents who taught me that hard work nearly always pays; to Andrew, who taught me both what is most funny and most true; and to Heidi and Henry for their love, support, perspective, and for bringing me the most natural smiles.

And of course, thanks to David Hardy, whose research has now helped build a movement that can't ever be silenced.

JASON CLARKE